AFROPOLITANISM
AND
THE BLACK BLOGOSPHERE

Christelle Kedi

Afropolitanism
and
the black blogosphere

Edited by Halimat Shode and Nigel Watt

Publisher: Books of Africa Limited
16 Overhill Road
East Dulwich, London
SE22 0PH
United Kingdom

Web site: www.booksofafrica.com
Emails: admin@booksofafrica.com
sales@booksofafrica.com

Cover design by Sally Shitaake (graphism)
and Nadya Aissa (photography)

Copyright: © C. Kedi 2016

ISBN: 978-0-9935036-1-0

A CIP catalogue record for this book is available from the British Library

Printed in the UK by

Contents

PART III

CASE STUDIES AND PORTRAITS

General Introduction

What is a blog? The word in itself is a contraction of two words: "web" and "log". They were both used by American John Barger, the original blogger in 1997. To describe his activity of "logging the web", Barger started using the term "blog". An alternative source claims that another early blogger, Peter Merholz, created the word in 1999 when describing his activity of online writing for a community.

The blogosphere has become part of the media know-how enabling the direct feedback from consumers of products, readers of content and viewers. Investigating its mechanisms and specificities within an "Afropean" scene is the aim of this book.

According to the article, "Social media: Beauty and Personal Care"[1] the Internet has become a total part of the consumer's experience. Discussions, recommendations, endorsements, opinions and tastes have become valuable to brands creating a leading and major role for the opinion sharing experience as a whole. Meanwhile the development of social networks throughout the late 90s has changed the definition of friendship therefore enabling the disappearance of geographical barriers and time limitations. The world is smaller and accessible 24 hours a day via the Internet.

Being at the heart of significant alteration in consumer behaviour, the Internet now faces more educated users with beauty concerns. This tool is used nowadays as a powerful and time saving option to research about products, reviews and expertise. As a consequence, the customer has become a powerful force to be considered by the

---

1. The quick expert guide to writing a blog (2012) Plaja, Luisa, p. 6-7.

beauty and fashion industries. Black people are no exception: the sophistication of web development has led to a huge increase in quality among black beauty blogs. Both the functionality and visuals have become equally important for attracting followers and readers. These facts have nourished the emergence of a new driving force within the comprehension of consumers' behaviour and communication within specific communities and niche groups. Successful black online platforms have flourished as fast as their white counterparts in the Americas, Africa and Europe. Some of these blogs have become as influential as traditional media. They share news in specialist areas and influence regarding people's lifestyle decisions. For Catherine Knight Steele, one of the first academics to have investigated the Black blogging practice in the USA, Black blogging is always political whether deliberately or not[2]. Since gossip about black celebrities informs many community forums and chats, numerous members of society are scrutinized by invisible members of large online groups.

Antoinette Pool (an academic who wrote the first PhD dissertation around the subject of Black political blogging) and Catherine Steel: female black blogging is a dissident act to resist various types of oppression[3] including:

- Physical oppression
- Personal oppression
- Communal oppression
- Institutionalized oppression

It is understandable that black female online groups prefer blogging to community environments where several factors, including time, might challenge some of them in their opinion sharing experience. With easy access and the anonymity factor on the Internet,

---

2. Steele, C.K. (2012) Blogging While Black: a critical analysis of resistance discourse by black female bloggers.
3. McKenna, Laura and Antoinette Pole. "Do Blogs Matter? Weblogs in American Politics." Presented at the American Political Science Association's Annual Meeting. Chicago, IL. September 2004.

black people as a whole seem less reluctant to discuss issues related to them. In the safety and comfort of their homes, black people can enjoy discussing with peers located anywhere in the world issues that are considered important to them.

In USA-based Black communities, high-speed interconnection has benefited E-commerce, F-commerce[4] and M-commerce[5]. These commercial practices are the direct result of communication using Internet as the main tool.

Making Black bloggers' sites more effective to use as both commercial platforms and forums for quality comparisons and community news has also benefited the dissemination of information related to manufacturers of cosmetics for an African-American buyer pool. Multinationals can now obtain a more accurate understanding of their customer's needs. Consequently, they can target their consumers more efficiently. Nevertheless, the Internet revolution has shown some limitations to its use. Online security, pornography, cyber criminality, data protection and misinformation are among the most harmful challenges that both communities and governments have to overcome to improve the virtual experience.

The entire media industry has also significantly witnessed the consequences of online activity mixing journalism with what Andrew Keen would call "citizen journalism"[6]: untrained people sharing news when having access to either information or resources to investigate a subject using journalistic approaches and methodologies. The main difference between the two types of practice is that citizen journalists are not responsible for their writings while journalists are.

One reality is that online activity is largely dominated by the blogosphere. Described as: "genres of texts defined not so much by their form or content as by the kinds of uses to which they are put, and the ways these uses construct social identities and communities"[7], blogs

---

4. Facebook commerce
5. Mobile commerce.
6. The Cult of the Amateur: How Today's Internet Is Killing Our Culture (2007).
7. The Discourse of Blogs and Wikis (2009).

are a mixture of memoir and graphic novel[8]. They inherited ethno-photography practices and photojournalism tools. However, in that climate of fast information and awareness among consumers, the Black consumer market as a whole has recently experienced the birth of a new stardom. This phenomenon has enabled serious business leads to both *beautypreneurs*[9] and *fashionpreneurs*[10]. Opinion leaders have also burgeoned out of this Internet scene. Described as "influential members of a community, group, or society to whom others turn for advice, opinions, and views". Opinion leaders are also perceived "as a minority group (early adopters) that passes information on new products [received from both media and manufacturers] to less trendy people (late adopters or the majority)". Most Black blogs in Europe do influence Black people by using both methods of information sharing and endorsements from manufacturers. Some are clearly explaining and assuming their roles between the consumers who listen to them and the manufacturers who pay them. Others are embarrassed by the situation of being listened to by both their readers and multinationals in need of a better profiling of their potential pool of buyers. Nevertheless, the role of these trend setters is clearly to support the identification of needs within a specific market, using their personal image as a reference to convince their followers: the industry members and general public.

We could say that the Black and European-based blogosphere has largely embraced the culture of ego-casting[11]. Following trends set by their US-located counterparts, stardom status for a Black blogger is for many a sign of achievement. It represents either an opportunity to stand out as an online leader or as a real life opinion shaper. In all cases, business is a main consideration. Therefore, the culture of self-promotion among these online personalities is common as well as ego-casting. Ego-casting, defined as the sharing of personal information or privacy using instant and online photo novellas, has directed the Internet revolution into new areas. Ego-casting is responsible for

---

8. The Discourse of Blogs and Wikis (2009).
9. Beauty entrepreneurs.
10. Fashion entrepreneurs.
11. The Cult of the Amateur: How Today's Internet Is Killing Our Culture (2007).

the development of online opinion sharers and leaders. When considering selfies[12] on Black-orientated online platforms or blogs or social media, they are no exception. Photographs, pictures and signs are all visual semiotics, as explained by Jonathan Bignell[13]: "[...] semiotics take the way that language works as the model for all other media of communication, all other sign systems" via "citizen journalism". This has expanded exponentially in regard to the success of platforms such as *Instagram*, *Youtube* or *Wikipedia*.

In her 2005 journal article about the Black Bloggers and the Blogosphere, Dr Antoinette Pole has interviewed 20 Black bloggers from the US Internet scene. She assesses how Black bloggers use their medium to influence politics. She also assessed whether Black bloggers were facing online discrimination from their fellow White bloggers. Her findings include the lack of discrimination among Internet-based black opinion leaders and a real participation in the political engagement they create amongst their readers and followers. Dr Pole describes blogs as "online diaries updated on daily basis, displayed in reverse-chronological order." Among her results, some are relevant to the role of Black blogs in general despite the study being outdated in terms of Internet consumption, the analysis could be paralleled with the European-based leading black beauty, fashion and lifestyle blogosphere:

• Black bloggers are more likely to blog about issues related to race and ethnicity than their counterparts from non-minority bloggers (McKenna and Pole 2006)

• Similarly, White bloggers are not likely to share the specific content of Black bloggers because they write about issues that involve the overall population not probing how other matters may impact minorities

White beauty/fashion/lifestyle bloggers do not have the same rapport to beauty/fashion/lifestyle than their black counterparts

---

12. Auto-portraits of self, using smart mobile phones or technology.
13. Media semiotics (1997).

since their priorities are different. The desire for eternal youth, for status symbols and following trends is likely to develop a tendency to over-produce changes in lifestyles and habits in order to make various claims. This phenomenon has been observed through:

- Trending (beauty and fashion latest European options)
- Health and Beauty trends
- Travel
- Diet management

Black bloggers in general (who will be presented geographically in the final part of this book) have a propensity for extensive conversations about:

- Daily hair care
- The latest beauty and fashion options in America
- Black cultures and societies
- Travels

This is a consequence of being physically and culturally different while being absorbed by a socio-ethnic and geographical majority.

To properly understand the black European-based beauty, fashion and lifestyle blogosphere phenomenon, we researched how much information was available about blogs in general. Since our area of investigation was chosen according to our personal and professional experiences in France and the United Kingdom, we chose to evaluate the impact of Black and European based online platforms in fashion cities in the northern hemisphere, London and Paris primarily.

While most of the academic and industrial analyses were targeting the US-based blogosphere to acknowledge the global black online experience, close to no information about wired activities by African communities in Europe was evaluated. Not to mention that books dedicated to fashion blogs around the world never mentioned successful black blogs.

What about the Black bloggers in Europe? Are they influencing the trends among their communities? Where do they originate? Where do they live? What are they talking about? Are they popular? Can their popularity be measured? Are they successful? Why are they invisible to the industry they talk about?

Afropolitanism is defined in the first chapter below. Initially searching for Afropolitan styles in Europe and its dissemination for a trend report, we decided to focus the exploration both online and offline, therefore including the Black European leading fashion and lifestyle blogosphere.

The primary data for this book was collected through surveys, interviews, observations and focus groups with 25 black bloggers 9 of whom are men and women in European countries including Belgium, France, Finland, Germany, Italy, Luxembourg, Portugal, Sweden, Switzerland and the United Kingdom. 21 bloggers responded to the surveys and another 5 bloggers were willing to share their experiences on the telephone so as to gain a deeper understanding of their motivations. The focus groups were conducted between November 2013 and February 2014 while the interviews and online surveys were organised between March and July 2014. The blogs were selected according to:

- their longevity (at least 2/3 years of continuous online activity)
- visual semiotics (logo and design of the platform)
- content (quality of information, its source and dissemination)
- online visibility/popularity
- readership
- potential economic growth
- Location

The business tools to evaluate the e-marketing strategies were:
- SWOT matrix
- PESTEL
- Ansoff matrix

The socio-cultural elements to assess the blogs were:

- Country of residence
- Country of origin
- Online platform's speciality or interest
- Local (history of black people
- Age
- Gender

Part I

Black trend setters
in European fashion cities

Chapter I
Being a Trendy Black European

1. United Kingdom: the history of Afropolitan identity

The original term *Afropolitanism* was used the very first time by Tuakli-Worsonu also known as Taiye Selasi (2005)[14]1: "You'll know us by our funny blend of London fashion, New York jargon, African ethics, and academic successes. Some of us are ethnic mixes, e.g. Ghanaian and Canadian, Nigerian and Swiss; others merely cultural mutts".

Leora Farber (2010)[15] describes *Afropolitanism* in fashion and fashion design as: "the field of fashion and its propagators is firmly interwoven into the social and economic fabric of design." She then goes on to reference South Africa regarding Afropolitanism, "beginning to contribute to the reorganisation of socio-cultural and economic life in this post-apartheid South Africa. It seems to be the case that South African fashion entry, by foregrounding South Africa's contemporary cultural heterogeneity, effectively marketing a range of creatively "African" fashion garments, and enhancing the market-oriented and socio-cultural positions of fashion design and propagators thereof in local and global fashion markets. "

---

14. « Selasi » Tuakli-Wosornu, Taiye (2005). Bye-Bye, Babar (Or: What is an Afropolitan?).
15. Farber, L. (2010). Stepping out in hybrid style: re-negotiating and re-imagining identities in contemporary South African fashion design. Cultural economy in contemporary South Africa: consumption, commodities and media. Guest edited by S Narunsky-Laden. Critical Arts 24(1), March: 128-167.

Chielozona Eze (2014)[16] explains and "V.Y. Mudimbe (1988)[17] has argued that Africa is an invention of the West, and Kandiatu Kanneh (1998)[18] has demonstrated that Africa has been reinvented by peoples of African descent. [...]. In 2005, Taiye Selasi coined the word *Afropolitanism* as a means to explain her own complex identity melange. Since then the term has gained some currency in African discourse of culture and politics.

"[...] *Afropolitanism* has to be primarily understood for what it is: an effort to grasp the diverse nature of being African or of African descent in the world today." The meaning of being *Afropolitan* to Black British people of an earlier generation, may be different to what a Black Londoner of today would experience. As mentioned by Louise from Afroblush, one of the blogs we investigated, "Afropolitan people are people who are familiar with Africa therefore born there". For Louise from LouiseSamPhotography.com, "Afropolitan identity is a reduction of self into a limited dimension, eventually out casting and excluding others; specifically those living in countryside". There are various definitions of the true meaning of Afropolitanism.

What does it mean to be an Afropolitan? How does lifestyle and history inform Afropolitanism? This can be traced back to what it means to be Black British. To better understand the development of this concept these last 10 years, I will give a short introduction to the local (fashion) history of Black people in the UK.

Largely originating from ex-British African colonies and the West Indies, the Black minority in Britain has had a long tradition of presence on this island. As recently seen at the Black Cultural archives, the black cultural heritage centre in Brixton, South London, the first black woman to have been buried on the British soil was of North African origin and lived thousands of years ago. As mentioned

---

16. Eze, Chielozona (2014) Rethinking African culture and identity: the Afropolitan model, Journal of African Cultural Studies 26 (2), 234-247.
17. Mudimbe, V.Y. (1988)The Invention of Africa. Gnosis, Philosophy, and the. Order of Knowledge, Bloomington, Indiana University Press.
18. Kanneh, Kandiatu (1998) African Identities: Race, Nation and Culture in Ethnography, Pan-Africanism and Black Literatures.

by Dr Kaufmann[19] who investigated the African presence in Great Britain[20] for her Oxford thesis, "diplomatic relations with Africa and a concomitant increased level of contact with Africans in the Atlantic world" allowed Black people who "came from Africa to train as trade factors and interpreters for English merchants [...] in the entourages of royals, gentlemen or foreign merchants". She later mentioned that: "They performed a wide range of skilled roles and were remunerated in the same mix of wage, reward and gifts in kind as others. They were accepted into society, into which they were baptized, married and buried. They inter-married with the local population and had children. Africans accused of fornication and men who fathered illegitimate children with African women were punished in the same way as others." In today's world, many Black British remember the difficult times their great parents or forefathers had when thinking they were the first to encounter Europeans either in a hostile Caribbean environment in the early 20th century or in Europe when they landed to emigrate.

An unchallenged belief for a vast majority of people was that Black British history started 500 years ago. Elements to enforce that belief include the lack of traces of the African presence and ancestry in the UK: too few Black people can claim to have been the offspring of Africans who landed in the British Isles in the first centuries CE. If these Africans have descendants, they are likely no longer to be related to the present day Black British community. Subsequently, the recent debates among Black cultural organisations such as Black History Walks[21] about the "Gentrification of Peckham and Black areas[22]"2 introduced the history of the Black presence in the UK. Some records mentioning the death of the Roman emperor Septimius Severus, who was of African origin, in York in 211CE[23] are available at the British

19. PhD thesis 'Africans in Britain, 1500-1640 by Dr Miranda Kaufman (2011).
20. PhD thesis 'Africans in Britain, 1500-1640 by Dr Miranda Kaufman (2011).
21. www.blackhistorywalks.co.uk
22. http://blackhistorywalks.co.uk/index.php/talks-96/414-the-gentrification-of-peckham-and-other-black-areas
23. Birley, Anthony. Septimius Severus: The African Emperor. Garden City: Doubleday (1972) and Rashidi, Runoko. Black Star: The African Presence in Early Europe. London: Books of Africa (2011).

Museum. The expulsion from England of Black people, who had become numerous and prosperous, ordered by Queen Elizabeth I in 1601[24], reinforces the argument that Black people were living in the UK at that time. They were not all slaves and therefore may have not needed to identify themselves with anywhere but Africa. Today people from various "Black" backgrounds form about 3.3% of the population of England and Wales.[25]

Ethnic minority groups, England and Wales, 2011[1]		
England and Wales	Percentages	
White	Irish	0.9
	Gypsy or Irish Traveller	0.1
	Other White	4.4
Mixed/ multiple ethnic groups	White and Black Caribbean	0.8
	White and Asian	0.6
	White and Black African	0.3
	Other Mixed	0.5
Asian/Asian British	Indian	2.5
	Pakistani	2.0
	Bangladeshi	0.8

24. http://www.nationalarchives.gov.uk/pathways/blackhistory/early_times/elizabeth.htm
25. Census 2011, Office for National Statistics.

	Chinese	0.7
	Other Asian	1.5
Black/ African/ Caribbean /Black British	African	1.8
	Caribbean	1.1
	Other Black	0.5
Other ethnic group	Arab	0.4
	Any other ethnic group	0.6
1. This chart excludes White British (80.5 per cent)		
Source: Census 2011, Office for National Statistics		

Ethnic groups, England and Wales, 2011		
England and Wales	Percentages	
White	86.0	
Mixed/ Multiple Ethnic Groups	2.2	
Asian/Asian British	7.5	
Black/African/Caribbean/Black British	3.3	
Other Ethnic Group	1.0	
Source: Census 2011, Office for National Statistics		

Some Black people may confirm that their West Indian heritage and identity dates back to the period of transatlantic slavery. Not always taking into account the history of deported Africans or as stated earlier, those who came to Europe out of curiosity for business opportunities, training or political and diplomatic affiliations. In all cases, these first black settlers were never called "*Afropolitans*" despite being Africans living in big cities often for the rest of their lives while intermarrying. Globalization was not as extensive then but it was already present in trade, exchange and culture. The difference is the technology used nowadays to keep ourselves aware of contemporary challenges and this difference has increased since the Internet revolution.

Defining *Afropolitans* based on current socio-geographical situations (mainly acculturation and mixed identities) may have some historical inaccuracy since the phenomenon was not new. Widening that designation into a fashion context may be challenging. *Afropolitan* fashion is associated with acknowledging a mixed cultural heritage born from a capacity of being African and cosmopolitan at the same time[26]. *Afropolitan* fashion might also mean being an African out of the continent but still aware of its societies and values. Therefore what is being cosmopolitan? Is it applicable to the African Diaspora, people who have not chosen to be geographically dispersed? Stuart Hall[27] defined the Caribbean propensity to outline its multiculturalism or plural identity in regard to two main characteristics:

- Identity as "the essence of 'Caribbeanness', of black experience"
- Identity as "discontinuities"

In the first concept, being Caribbean emphasises the idea of having to recreate an identity due to a community reawakening after the traumas experienced over recent centuries by West Indians of African extraction. In the second concept, Stuart Hall acknowledges three different types of discontinuities when claiming Caribbean identity:

- The identity created by the colonial power
- The identity created by the *Creolization* effect

26. Kedi, Christelle (2014) interviews blogger Afroblush (2014)
27. Hall, S. (1993) Cultural identity and Diaspora. London.

- The identity created when returning to the Caribbean after the experience in England.

When analysing these three notions, the last identity is closest to "*Afropolitanism*". Experiencing England for the very first time as a large group has been largely investigated by Paul Gilroy and by Hall. "Black Britishness" is defined by Hall as being a creation, a narrative of an individual and how he perceives him/herself. It is a choice. The creation of a Creole identity is the consequence of the *Creolization* process which will be elaborated on in the next section. Identity in this case results from deported Africans or colonised Africans from specific areas including Cape Verde or Brazil lacking cultural references from their past.

The identity created by the colonial power often referred to the nationalism or nationality provoked by resistance to colonialism. This identity often fails to recall that parts of the African continent and the West Indies were renamed, repossessed and rebranded several times by different colonial powers before the creation of the states we know today. When making an allowance for the British Caribbean *Creolization* process, Kenneth Morgan concedes the "demographic composition of the slave population shaped the parameters of slave life [...] in the Caribbean"[28] and created opportunities of *multiculturalism* as an educational alternative. In his examples, the professor compares the colonial USA with both Barbados and Jamaica. As young black men and teenagers were sought after during the transatlantic slave trade by British slave owners, Kenneth Morgan explains that the situation was different in North America. There, slave owners had a majority of indentured servants born in United States. This limited the influx of Africans, who were judged too difficult to manage culturally, emotionally, physically and spiritually.

These Africa-born captives were likely to be rebellious and to catch local diseases (as their bodies could not cope with the new climate and diet and they were traumatised by the middle passage in which they witnessed death, misery and extreme conditions.

---

28. Morgan, Kenneth (2010) The Oxford History of Britain (1987, rev ed 2010).

Consequently, American colonisers also noticed a higher birth rate among America-born black women. Americans were among the first to bring displaced African women to the New World. Most deported Africans arrived in America before 1750, hence creating a *Creole* culture earlier than elsewhere. British colonisers in the Caribbean compensated for the high death rate among African male slaves by importing more of them. Subsequently the first generations of Black *Creoles* appeared respectively from 1810 in Barbados and 1840 in Jamaica. The extreme conditions of life in the Caribbean for Africans had a serious impact on reproduction. British slave owners witnessed the reluctance for Creole female slaves to get pregnant as the mortality was extremely high among infants (50%) and they were not permitted any time to develop safe pregnancies. Miscarriages and lack of menstruation were common. African women were likely to get impregnated but would breastfeed their children until the age of three as an attempt to control births. In that context, our hypothesis would be that women in the British Caribbean as early as the 19th century took the lead in terms of family development and culture. These women transmitted their *Creole* knowledge of self which has been passed down ever since. This massive *creolization* around the end of transatlantic slave trade in the British Caribbean led to the birth of a mixed culture.

Building or reconstructing a local identity was based on life experience, affected by the differences between the colonial powers. Being *Creole* was seen as being better than being African. Nowadays, this is still the case for many Afro-Caribbeans; for them, being named *Afropolitan, Black British, Black European* or *Black French* is better than being called *African* especially when they have not been born in Africa. Black Africans born out of Africa are no exception to this rule. In a recent conversation with several leading black bloggers from continental Europe it was astonishing that they did not wish to be defined as "*Afropolitan*". Some were familiar with the word, associating it with a cosmopolitan lifestyle for Africans, while others found it restrictive to a minority of "Africans". *Afropolitanism* can take several forms, shapes and definitions, but for the purpose of our analysis we will now focus on its significance in fashion terms.

2. Black hierarchy of influence

This hypothesis of the Black hierarchy of influence may only apply to the world of fashion icon construction. This assumption is based on the amount of exposure given to Black men and women across online media dedicated to fashion and as read within the blogs investigated. Their content mostly relates to the realities of different Black presence around the world. The most spoken about remain the Black Americans. Presented as the most sophisticated and Westernized of Black people in the modern world, African-Americans represent the achievement of the "civilizing mission" of the European 19th century theories of Gobineau (1816-1882) and Darwin (1809-1882).

Barely comprising 5% of the worldwide Black community, they are over-represented in the global media[29]. However, the Americans differ from their European counterparts in the type of migration which settled them in the northern hemisphere. The reason for their presence in the USA is another element of differentiation, and important movements created by African-Americans such as the civil rights movement have shown unity in their common goals. Physical differences were, and still are, the only basis of discrimination. Their history as enslaved Africans badly affected their image in America, as people of African origin. Both emancipation and recognition of their identity were vital to the Black community in the USA.

The other Black communities worldwide developed cultures and nations based on lands in which they were either a majority (the Caribbean and Africa) or a large minority (Brazil). Their demands and struggles were adapted to their environment: economic equality and job opportunities, eradication of racially-based divisions in society and freedom of speech and religious practice. The hierarchy of influence is about understanding how the Black European blogosphere has largely inherited communication codes and social needs resulting from the way Blacks were regarded in colonial times. Black communities in Europe seem to have inherited a way of codifying

---

29. C. Kedi, Beautifying the body in ancient Africa and today (2013).

colonial values as well as the system of social classes. Hall explained the Creolization process for the first generations of Black Caribbeans in the UK, and he also explores the complexity of being Black European fed by a Westernized depiction of self. After defining Afropolitan, we can look at what it means is being "Black" today.

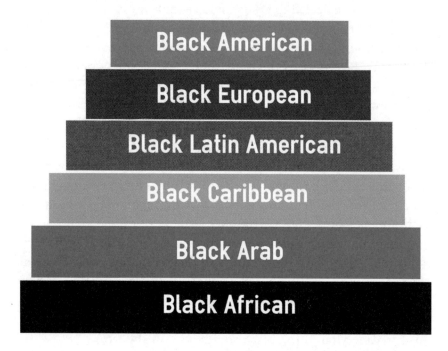

As the second largest influential group: the Black Europeans are mainly migrants from the Caribbean and Africa. This geographical and cultural group is perceived as those who have been exposed to the "most civilized" part of the contemporary world, Europe. As mentioned by Diop[30], the first generations of educated Blacks in Europe were likely to be: "[…] deeply affected […] [by] the world opinion about him and his people". That intellectual would lose his confidence in his own personal abilities and would hardly be "victimized by this alienation

---

30. Diop, Cheikh Anta (1987) Precolonial Black Africa: a comparative study of the political and social systems of Europe and Black Africa, from antiquity to the formation of modern states.

[…] that they seek to codify"[31]. Regarded as role models by their relatives who remained "back home", Black Europeans, especially the first generation of migrants, were keen to be compared to their US-peers.

Since the Harlem Renaissance in the 1920s, Black Europeans have identified themselves with the African-American struggle for civil rights and racial equality. For our purposes we will divide them into two types. The first group of bloggers, the "naturalized", as described by Hall, consists of those who have experienced a social downturn since they found it hard to find the sort of positions they had held in their own countries when they migrated to Europe. Some may have made up for this by wearing "fine clothes as a means of financial comfort."[32] The second group, those "born here" are the largest group represented among the Black bloggers: their parents and elders, the "naturalized," have in most cases brought them up to believe that they belong exclusively either to their motherland or to Europe, not to both. Why? In both cases, the African identity was forged by personal experience rather than by community or group experience as in the case of the African-Americans. From a Caribbean background, a young person would inherit codes of identification based on nationality: Barbadian, Guyanese or other. When among people from the same location, they would identify by town or village. When they come from the same town or village, they would be identified by social class. These three components combine to produce people with a similar culture but with different interests.

Black Caribbeans did not all arrive in Europe at the same time or under the same conditions. The first Black Caribbean migrants in France arrived in the early 20th century. They were mainly descended either from mixed-raced families or generations of free people who had set up as business owners and civil servants. They came to France and Paris in particular either to study or to travel for social and

31. Diop, Cheikh Anta(1987) Precolonial Black Africa: a comparative study of the political and social systems of Europe and Black Africa, from antiquity to the formation of modern states.
32. Diop, Cheikh Anta(1987) Precolonial Black Africa: a comparative study of the political and social systems of Europe and Black Africa, from antiquity to the formation of modern states.

educational purposes or for pleasure. At that time well to do young people had to be "launched" into society in Paris rather than in the provinces or in the colonies. The second generation arrived with the world wars inspiring people such as Frantz Fanon[33], to describe the reasons why he enrolled in the French army. His generation, who brought the Harlem Renaissance to Paris, was also educated and financially comfortable. They were aspiring to develop and find out about the "*Metropole*", the Motherland.

The third wave of Caribbean migrants to France was in the 1960's to 1970s with the *Bumidom,* a controversial institution set up by the French government in 1962 to supply French industry with cheap labour from French Overseas Departments. The migration was controversial because people were offered a bright future but regardless of the level of their education they, along with African migrants, were supposed to take jobs that indigenous French people refused to take, such as in post offices and hospitals.

This identity situation also shows a valuable cultural element of differentiation. In the case of Black French from the Caribbean, their reality was nourished by the difficulty of blending into one single Black experience in Europe. Within their own communities, skin tone disparities and socio-economic backgrounds reinforced by many years of isolation and submission to a colonial power, left them socially divided. Their offspring, the second and third generations had to manage these identity challenges while at the same time having both to adapt and adopt a Eurocentric view of self. This is true for both the "naturalized" and the "born here". For indigenous French people, these *Blacks* were all the same!

An example is described by Selasi (2005) and Miano[34], the former born in England and the second having migrated to France from Cameroon. Different times, life options and motivations led the two authors to experience similar circumstances. For both writers, the personal understanding of self was largely influenced by the

---

33. Franz Fanon (1925-1961) Black Skin, White Masks (1952), (1967) translation by Charles Lam Markmann: New York: Grove Press.
34. Miano, Leonora (2008) Afropean soul.

original ethnic community to which they belonged, together with the national identity they developed as Black women. For Selasi, she is "Black British", a child of West African parents who migrated to UK several decades ago. Miano qualifies as Black French, since she chose to leave her country to study in France as her social background motivated her to do. The two women have developed an Afrocentric perspective of self. In response to the question: what is being African, for Selasi it is a consequence of a personal journey, specifically multi-cultural in her case. For Miano, it is introspection about how Africa is perceived by Africans themselves in Africa and in the diaspora. The success of these two women writers for Black Europeans and Black Africans is understandable. They raise identity questions that generations of Black Europeans have been asking ever since they had to adapt to living as a minority within a nation who has judged their communities according to their history. Many bloggers use the word diaspora in their online work since that term seems to unite people: most Black Europeans consider themselves to be part of it. However, diaspora is defined by African Union as people who are living in a land to which they were forced to migrate.

Afrocentrism, the response to being a reconstructed minority within a nation with a long history, seems to be temporary main road to overcome social prejudices. Understanding self through the eye of another culture might be confused by the imagery and words used to describe their original ethnicity: "Black", « Noir », « natu-ralisée », « sans papiers », "illegal immigrant", "economic migrant", "refugee", "Antillais", "Coloured", « Personne de couleur », "West Indian", "Caribbean", and especially "African". "African" is associated by some people with negative images of violence, lack of respect, lack of organisation, moral and social poverty and cultural deprivation.

If we apply some of Bourdieu's[35] reflections about the socio-economic impact of culture in the social space occupied by individuals and, by extension, social groups, the cultural capital is a consequence of both social and economic capital. For these two women, despite

35. Bourdieu, Pierre (1979) Distinction.

not being indigenous to Europe, the hardship of belonging to a community of economic migrants has empowered them in the context of European cultural domination. They were eager to achieve in this unfamiliar environment. Introspection became the quickest way of gaining a positive image of themselves. At the time, most of the represented, successful and positive role models in Western media were African-Americans in television series such as the *Cosby Show*. This is where the influence of America can be perceived as a starting point in the cultural domination of these Black Europeans.

Black America had, long before Black Europeans' lifestyles were investigated, clearly assimilated lifestyle options. Black Americans offered an essential alternative to the second generation of Afro-Caribbeans in Europe. Since Black Americans were all "born in the USA", they represent a minority within a Western society dominated by European-Americans. Black Europeans "born here" (as they enjoy mentioning in London and especially in Paris) believe they can be assimilated or at least perceived as equivalent to their US peers. In both their social challenges and their dreams they try to match those of African-Americans despite their new status as "Europeans". Blacks were living in Europe hundreds of years ago but how many of these "born here" can trace back their blood lines to these Africans?

The other part of the African diaspora deported to the Americas, the Black Latin Americans, including Brazilians, Colombians and Peruvians and the Black Caribbeans are still often more popular in the Western world and in Africa than Africans themselves. The reason being the "myth related to the positive *Creolization* process" which is defended by the mainstream media, by government in these countries and through cultural propaganda. In reality, if we take the example of Brazil, the racially mixed society was created and largely encouraged by the Portuguese monarchy and governments throughout the 500 years of transatlantic slave history. The whiter a person was, the purer the individual was perceived to be. Their economic and social freedom was attached to their skin colour. It is interesting to look at both the Brazilian and Cuban societies before the development of sugar plantations in the 18th century. Among the first lands to have been colonised by Iberian populations from Europe, Cuba and Brazil, were multiracial. Numbers in Cuba suggested that in 1775, the non-whites represented 20% of the total population and 41% were free people[36]. Largely under-researched, the history of Blacks in Cuba for example is a long story of physical denial, violence (riots in 1912) and resistance accompanied by the preservation of their original religions, *Santeria* and *Abakua*. The first is an offspring of the traditional Yoruba practices while the second is an all-male secret society originating from Cameroon and Nigeria. This fraternity has largely spread its influence into the numerous contemporary Cuban dances. Dance was used as a means of communication among Blacks before the end of slavery in Cuba. The *Partido Independiente de Color* was created in 1908 after the treatment inflicted by white Cubans on their Black peers during the Cuban War of Independence against Spain. Slavery was abolished in 1886 in Cuba, the last island in America to have done so, only to be survived by a US-type of apartheid resulting from the entrance of Americans into the Spanish-American War in 1898. In May 1912, at the peak of the conflicts opposing Whites and Blacks in Cuba for a fairer representation of all citizens in the newly formed government, the Cuban race war started against the odds. Supported by the Americans settled on the island, the government brutally assaulted thousands of Afro-Cubans, many unarmed, in an effort to imitate the Brazilian policy of "whitening the nation" by importing more Europeans and the USA's racially divided society[37]. For governments such as those in Brazil and Cuba, "whitening" society was about supressing the physical evidence of a Black presence using propaganda in favour of mixed-couples. The establishment of a brutal racially-based system of ghettos to create the social and economic dismembering of an entire community was also a popular method of "whitening"[38]. Isolated, the Blacks were more likely to be located in certain areas and eventually attacked if necessary.

The lifestyle conditions of Black Cubans in the first part of the 20th century are well described by Nicola Guillen (1902-1989).

36. The Caribbean by Gad Heuman (2006) p. 36.
37. General history of the Caribbean, edited by Bridget Brereson, Unesco, p. 230-234.
38. A concise history of Brazil by Boris Fausto (1999), pp. 118-120.

The *Creolization* process in Black Latin America is sometimes wrongly branded as successful. As a result, the cultures born out of tragedy and pain are praised by those who tend to forget that this wonderful music is a consequence of a denial of spiritual and identity to Blacks in search of peace. To preserve their practices, Black Cubans and Black Brazilians hide their identity in their songs and dances. These hidden codes are nowadays popular in the global entertainment industry. Because of the untold stories of failed attempts to remove the African elements in both of these countries, a large mixed-race society was artificially created and marketed to the world, making the Black Latin American third in the hierarchy of Black influence.

Similarly Black Caribbeans are observed as "less indigenous" than Black Africans based on similar grounds to those affecting the previous groups. Looking back at the arrival of what we would call the "neither black nor white" syndrome, Heuman[39] writes that "Slavery was a complicated institution"[40]. Mainly made of settlers (Europeans), natives (Caribs), enslaved people (Africans, mixed-race and Caribbean) and free people (Africans, mixed-race and Caribbean), as seen earlier in the example of Black Latin America, society was extremely stratified in terms of race and gender. The settlers were mainly males while a majority of the enslaved people (depending on the island) were African and Caribbean males. Females were imported in big numbers to the French and British islands when the slave traders and the land owners as a response to the high death rate among slaves and the resulting number of physically threatening men. Only Caribbean born slaves or young children taken from Africa would eventually be seen as reliable, valuable and obedient slaves. They would be unlikely to try to overcome the colour-based society. As a result of sexual relationships between African women and European settlers, a generation of mixed-race people started to expand. Many were freed with their mothers by their European fathers leading to the growth of a mainly female-led free population. About 500 free people in Martinique in 1696 were

39. Heuman, Gad (2006) The Caribbean (Brief histories).
40. The Caribbean, Gad Heuman, Hodder Arnold (2006) p. 34.

registered out of 13,000 enslaved people while by 1789, 5,235 free people were counted compared to 83,414 enslaved[41].

The British, French, Spanish and Danish Caribbean islands had significant naming for the different types of people of colour. The case of an individual with a black and a white parent was named *"Mulatto"*; born from a black and a "mulatto" parent, the child was called *"Sambo"*; a *"quadroon"* was the child born from a *"mulatto"* and a white individual. A *"Mustee"* was born out of a *"quadroon"* and a white parent; the *"Musteefino"* was born out of a white individual and a *"mustee"* parent. Finally a *"Musteefino"* having a child with a white parent would give birth to a "white" child. Apart from the distinctions of colour, the way in which people were classified as free, differed from one another.

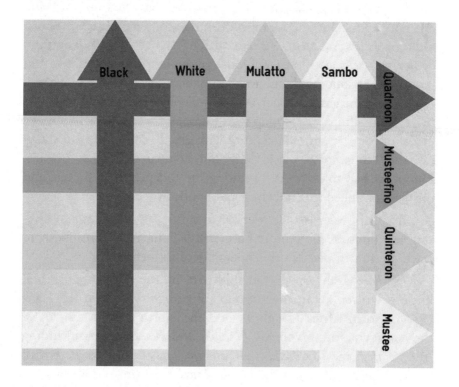

41. Neither Slave nor free: the Freedom of African descent in the slave societies of the New World, 1972 by Cohen and Greene, p. 335-339.

Some people were born free while some others were manumitted, emancipated. As a matter of fact, their rights were largely denied or at least very restricted. They could not always own land (in the French West Indies), they could not wear all types of clothes or fabric (in the Danish West Indies) or they could eventually revert into status of slaves (in the USA). We can now understand how the myth of the "superiority" of some people to others has lasted until the present affecting the perception that a Black European may have about self as an individual despite his geographical and historical origin. Skin tone and length of stay in a socio-geographical group was always (and still is) a marker of social capital among Blacks in general.

This attitude to skin colour is widespread across the Caribbean among Blacks and European settlers. Secondly, the presence of Europeans in significant numbers in all the Caribbean islands has acted as a "civilizing criterion" in making the region more attractive for tourists, investors, multi-nationals and media. As reminded by Archer-Straw: "Caricatures depicting blacks as colonial subjects, savage heathens, promoters and providers of exotic products, and entertainers gave Europeans a stock of ideas and images that black people were powerless to challenge [...] their race's shifting relationship with Europe"[42]. The role played by the media of the 19th and 20th century have greatly contributed to show-case the "exoticism" of Black Caribbeans compared to Black Africans. Europeans had to leave Africa during the Independence process and this has continued in Zimbabwe and South Africa.

Safer Caribbean islands friendly to European attitudes and offering less political discomfort have enabled the Black Caribbean to reach the fourth place in this hierarchy of influence.

The Afro-Arabs are a valuable part of the African Diaspora. Little is written about these groups of people. Found in the Sahel region, North Africa (Maghrib) and the North East (Mashreq) of the continent, the *Haranine*, *Gnawas* and *Black Berbers* including (the *Ketama*, the *Masmuda*, the *Sanhaja*, and the *Zenata Berbers* of coastal North Africa and the Upper Atlas) are from various but not

42. Archer-Straw, Petrine (2000) Negrophilia: Avant-Garde Paris and Black Culture in the 1920s.

diverse backgrounds. They are identified as Afro-Arabs for several reasons including: history, geography and language.

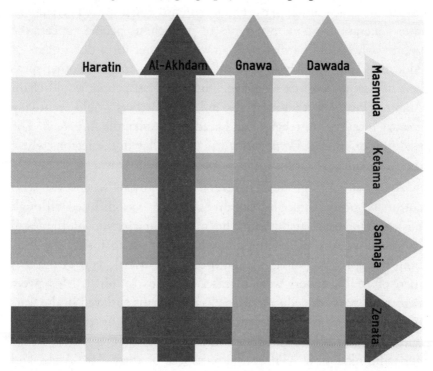

According to Oliver and Atmore[43], the word "Maghrib came from the Arabs when designating "Mediterranean lands west of Egypt", the far west comprised of Mauritania, Algeria and Morocco. Islam was established in that region in the 8th century to the extent that the existence of Latin Christianity in the area was forgotten. The Berber language was confined to the hinterland allowing the diffusion of Arabic language of communication among city people. Largely spread by Arab pastoralists named "*Banu Hilal*", these cultural ambassadors have "[...] traditionally been presented as a destructive element in *Maghribi* society." However, the *Banu Hilal*[44] was extensively encouraged by "[...] the policemen and the tax gatherers of the coast-based rulers, who

43. Medieval Africa 1250-1800 (2001) by Roland Oliver and Anthony Atmore (Cambridge University Press) pp. 32-48.
44. Medieval Africa 1250-1800 by Oliver and Atmore, p. 32.

rewarded them for their services with grants of land." These cultural and economic practices eventually opened the way for the dissemination of the Arab culture in the region, intensifying its power generation after generation. Soon, two types of indigenous people appear: the poorest who could hardly speak Arabic its purer form due to lack of education; and the richest, descendants of *Banu Hilal* and other speakers of Arabic as a first language. These well-off people would claim Arab origins. Nevertheless, Arabs and some Berbers would eventually create a local type of religious and academic leader, the *Marabout*. The tradition of visiting *Marabouts* is still alive today in the regions where the Afro-Arabs live and in Islamic parts of West Africa.

Arab colonisation allowed several racial groups to co-exist with culturally unity through religion[45]. Arabic was diffused through business and scholarship but the main characteristic of the Arab conquest was the use of the religious argument to justify the learning and spreading of Arabic culture. [For Oliver:] "Few of the first men of Arabic letters were themselves Arabs by birth. Most were descended from the educated Greeks or Persians enslaved in the wars of conquest, who were recruited as bureaucrats by the Umayyad and Abbasid Caliphs for their knowledge of earlier systems of law and administration." The physical aspect of these Afro-Arabs and their origins are still disputed despite recent DNA results. Pennell[46] clearly identified the Afro-Arabs as indigenous people who had been Islamised in the earliest years of Islam. Among them, the American Dr Dana Reynolds[47], who clearly identified the Afro-Arabs as indigenous people who have been Islamised as the earliest hours of the development of the Koranic religion. They were not to be confused with the descendants of captured Africans such as the *Gnawas*[48]

45. When we ruled (2006) by Robin Walker, p. 633-640.
46. Pennell, C. R. (2003) Morocco: From Empire to Independence.
47. The African heritage and ethnohistory of the Moors: Background to the emergence of early Berber and Arab peoples, from prehistory to the Islamic dynasties. in Journal of African Civilizations, Vol II, Fall 1991, pp. 93-150 by Dana R. Marcniche.
48. Les Noirs victimes du racisme au Maroc, Friday 27th May 2005, Afrik.com: http://www.afrik.com/article8447.html

in modern Morocco who are subject to local racism based on their level of integration into the dominant society. These Afro-Arab inhabitants are genetically linked to modern Malians and Senegalese and from Somali patriarchs who migrated centuries ago into the Atlas Mountains as also claimed by Tariq Berry[49] and academics such as Robert Davis[50]. Traditionally used in Morocco as soldiers, after Independence their status remained difficult as local society was still representing them as servants. Davis explores the mixing that took place in North Africa over the last 500 years or so as the result of trans-Mediterranean slave trade of European Christians and the trans-Saharan slave trade. These activities led East African communities (including the Somali from Berbera and the *Mangbetu* from Sudan) to move further west towards Central and North Africa to escape attacks by Arabs and Africans freshly converted to Islam.

These Afro-Arabs communities are related to the *Tuaregs,* sharing languages, customs and matriarchal societies. To be more precise, according to Diop[51], the original Nubians and surrounding communities moved further west to escape Arab and Persian invasions as well as the increasing drought in the region. These people part of the hierarchy of influences because their primarily nomadic cultures have been extensively researched. Understanding their mode of transmission of knowledge and historical records using their own alphabets as well as Arabic has contributed to the creation of a recognized set of written testimonies of academic value. Here, Africans could be considered accurate in the recording of their common traditions. Called sometimes the "Blue Men", Tuaregs have their annual festival held in Libya every October for the entire month. All the main groups acknowledge each other and meet to congregate and celebrate heritage, history and traditions. The *Ghadames* festival shares dances,

---

49. Berry, Tariq (2007) The Unknown Arabs: Clear, Definitive Proof Of the Dark Complexion Of the Original Arabs And the Arab Origin Of the So-Called African Americans.
50. Davis, Robert (2004) Christian Slaves, Muslim Masters: White Slavery in the Mediterranean, the Barbary Coast, and Italy, 1500-1800.
51. The African origin of civilization myth or reality (1974) by Cheikh Anta Diop, chapter IX, pp. 179 -186.

food and an opportunity to approach these communities, as did the writer and anthropologist Nabile Fares in 1969-1970 when he was writing his PhD thesis about the transmission of literature orally[52]. The Afro-Arabs occupy the place just above the Black Africans since they are already based in Africa. In the mind of many Black Europeans and their descendants, they are less exotic. They are associated with an Arabic culture since they use that language to write and communicate. They share the culture of the Arab world: a religious practice of culture. Nevertheless, they remain a nomadic minority among large majority of sedentary Africans.

Finally, Black Africans are at the bottom of this hierarchy (depending on how we read it) or they form last layer of influence on the Black European communities. Sometimes barely aware of the involvement and science behind customs and languages, Sub-Saharan Africans are widely victims of stereotypes often relayed by themselves. Typical examples within the fashion world are about the accreditation of wax as a sub-Saharan creation while the historical proof of its links to Dutch colonization of both Jakarta and West coast of Africa was openly presented in several exhibitions[53] in Paris. Another example is the widespread perception that sub-Saharan Africans did not have alphabets or history. In reality, both North and sub-Saharan Africans used "written" forms of records which were displayed on architecture, sculpture, textile, skin and hair as demonstrated in « Femmes, Genres et corps »[54]. The last example I will give but not the least is the false claim that most sub-Saharan traditional leaders were involved in both the trans-Saharan and the trans-Atlantic slave trades of Africans to Europe, Middle East, Asia and Americas. This claim has been deconstructed by several scholars including the first Portuguese settlers who visited Africa in the early 14th century. Gil Eanes (1395-?) who has been translated into English by Robert Kerr (1844) described

---

52. *Littérature orale et anthropologie,* thèse de Nabile Fares, janvier 1972 (Université de Paris X).
53. Pagne de campagne: géopolitique d'un tissu mondial (2015).
54. FIEGED Lyon October 2015.

how Portuguese and Arabs used to maintain entire villages as hostages in order to force the local authorities to cooperate with their deadly commerce. If the local leaders were opposing their wills, the entire villages would be taken into slavery to redeem the traders. These practices of forcing people to capture others in an attempt to make most profits for each sea crossing or sea expedition was documented by the Ancient Greeks selling North and East Europeans to slavery, John Byron (2003) and Junius P. Rodriguez (1997). Examples are: the selling of Europeans by the Ottoman Turks to Northern Africa which eventually led Europeans to fight the Ottomans in an attempt to stop the human trade, as in the bombardment of Algiers (1816); moors trading Christians in exchange for Muslim prisoners held in Europe or Africa (Richard Pennell 2003); the Code of Hammurabi (c 1750 BC); and finally Euro-Americans trading their own to settle in the New world (Don Jordan & Michael A. Walsh 2007).

The opinions or prejudices about Black Africans include a tendency to fight, for their governments to be corrupt, to be disorganised and not to be trusted. A lack of self-knowledge has resulted in a self-deprecation. Mistrust was generated by the sometimes hostile environment in which peoples had to define their identity. In many local wars people may have captured others just because they were not speaking the same language or practising the same religion. This story could be related to so many different parts of Sub-Saharan Africa. In Cameroon, as all along the coast of West Africa, coastal communities supported the trade in African slaves led by Portuguese, French and British in the 18th century. This trade did not involve the entire community but some leaders were greedy enough to think of ways to weaken the neighbouring nation in order to take over their lands and become more powerful. For example until today some communities in Cameroon continue to have some reserve when dealing with people from the coast.

The hierarchy of Black influence described above is a proposition to explore how Black Europeans are differently influenced by socio-geographically according to a perception of self often based on Western views or preferences of what is suitable in terms of "blackness" and what is not. Europe-based African trendsetters seem to be captivated by African-American dressing practices as a point of departure and as the peak of black fashion culture. Being "black" is a Western vision of delocalized and culturally-transformed Africans[55]. They do not know who they were before being moved to another country and as first generation arrivals they remained confused about their identity. They are too often ignorant of their history before colonial times. Therefore, they are often unwilling to accept being associated with Africa. In a recent general interest blog, an African-American woman travelling in Kenya was shocked to be asked by locals where she truly came from. The lady thought that because she had her direct ancestry mainly located and culturally associated with USA, she felt that she did not fit into that description of "African-American" since Irish-American or Italian-American had a link to their motherlands that her ancestors had lost[56]. The question we would enjoy asking to that woman is: "How could you compare your African ancestors who never chose to migrate to USA with those of Italians and Irish who decided to leave Europe because of economic hardship?" That woman explained only African migrants with American citizenship could qualify as "African-American". She defines herself as a "black American". Being "Black" means a dark skinned person for whom history started the day their ancestors reached the Western world for economic reasons: slave trade or lack of job opportunities. It is no surprise that the concept of being "*Afropolitan*" was born in "Black Europe" as we defined earlier.

3. Paris: Negritude and links to America and Africa

In what I call "Black hierarchy of influence" in fashion trends, Black Americans are a top of the pyramid. As specified by Christopher Breward[57]: "[...] the existence of certain cities with global status in the geographies of fashion [...]" seem to emphasize the legitimacy of what the same expert calls "[...] a long-established popular understanding

55. "What is Black history?" p. 20-45 in When we ruled (2006) by Robin Walker.
56. Slate.fr on 8th september 2014: http://www.slate.fr/story/90813/noir-americain-afro-americain
57. Breward, Christopher (2006) Fashion's World Cities (Cultures of Consumption Series).

of a certain urban hierarchy [...]". In the hierarchy of Black Cosmo-
politans, US-based Blacks are at the top of these African-orientated
global urban lifestyles. Furthermore, this state of mind and views about
African-Americans at the top of the global Black fashion hierarchy has
partly originated from the first Black French intellectual circles in the
early 20th century. Meeting for the very first time in Paris the "*Noirs
Américains*"[58] as they were called, Afro-Americans such as Richard
Wright (1908-1960), Langston Hughes (1902-1967) or Josephine
Baker (1906-1975) became inspirational to an entire generation of
Black French trend creators. In the his chapter "Celebrity and publicity
before Hollywood", Breward[59] describes the rise of icons as "[...] popular glorification of the luxurious lifestyles and habits of the rich relied
on the repeated description and reproduction of its details in gossip
columns, magazines, novels, paintings, theatre and latterly film [...]".
As a comparison, icons from the late 19th century and early 20th century
were widely promoted by photography, press and... fashion. Fashion
grew alongside celebrity culture, developing what Breward calls a
"fashion-orientated leader" or "style-leaders". Leaders of taste had the
responsibility to shape the aspirational lifestyle and trends of an entire
community. Afropolitanism is a similar movement. As we saw earlier,
Afropolitanism in a Black British context is a consequence of history,
culture and choice. Claiming that Afropolitan fashion is a result of
multiple influences in terms of identities is ultimately confessing differences in taste, interest and lifestyles. African and diaspora fashion is
rarely acknowledged by the international clothing industry as explained
by Carol Tulloch[60]. Meanwhile her Black British Style Exhibition tour[61]
confirmed that over half of the people who attended the exhibition in
Birmingham, Leicester and Sunderland, were Whites[62] and interested

58. Archer-Straw, Petrine (2000) Negrophilia: Avant-Garde Paris and Black Culture
in the 1920s.
59. Breward, Christopher (1995) The Culture of Fashion: A New History of
Fashionable Dress.
60. Tulloch, Dr Carol Professor of Dress, Diaspora and Transnationalism,
Camberwell, Chelsea, Wimbledon, University of the Arts.
61. Tulloch, Carol (2004) Black British Style Exhibition tour.
62. Tulloch, Carol (2004) Black British Style Exhibition tour.

to learn more about Black British Styles[63]. Consequently, fashion dissemination among African and Caribbean *fashionistos* or *fashionistas* is globally interrelated to its level of promotion and the imaging of self in the mainstream. This trend has led to the development of a campaign to have more Black models on European catwalks. This trend has also neglected understanding marketing strategies when broadcasting for a specific market located geographically, physically and culturally quite unlike the average African's appearance. Black Paris is no exception. I will try to clarify the major differences in experiencing African identities and stimuli in the world of universal Afropolitan fashion.

TREND MOVEMENT IN BLACK FASHION BLOGGING

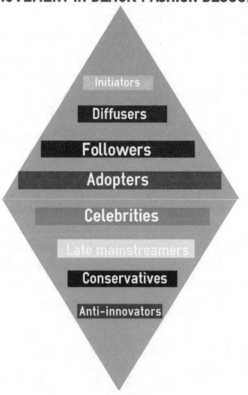

Initiators

Diffusers

Followers

Adopters

Celebrities

Late mainstreamers

Conservatives

Anti-innovators

Adapted diamond-shaped trend model[64]

---

63. Tulloch, Carol (2004) Black British Style Exhibition tour.
64. Adapted from www.henrikvejlgaard.com

The leaders of the *Négritude* movement were Aimé Césaire (1913-2008); Léon Gontran-Damas (1912-1978) and Léopold Sédar Senghor (1906-2001), supported by the Black French socialite, Paulette Nardal (1896-1985)[65] art lover Eugene Bullard (1895-1961) and a few others. They joined the Harlem Renaissance movement by including the Black American experience white supremacy in the USA into their demands for civil rights. They were visually motivated by the achievement and sophistication of the Black Americans. This attitude enabled the development of a Black US-based beauty myth surrounding Afro-Americans which has lasted until now. The myths according to Roland Barthes[66] are a "mode of signification, a form [...] to which should be assigned historical limits, conditions of use [...]". In other words, myths are a type of communication or speech: they include photography and moving images that both possess signifiers. Adapting signifiers to demographics and demo-geographics[67] is the essence of fashion promotion. That visual experience of elegantly styled, dressed and acclaimed « *Noirs Américains* » in early 20th century Paris by both Whites and Blacks, fed the example of being black and beautiful and "out of Africa". From that point, the typical African woman or man based in French speaking African or Caribbean countries aspired to become an identical version of his or her African-American equals, specifically the New York based Black elite. Since they could not imagine themselves wearing with diverse outfits unless in a historical or anthropological context, they inherited a version of what "black" beauty was. Today the cultural shift affecting both West Indians and Africans in France as they face every day the American depiction of self through the fashion pictures has not changed. Events such as the one pictured were organised in the heart of Paris (March 2014) and are branded successful as three out of four guests at their various events were Afro-Americans.

65. Archer-Straw, Petrine (2000) Negrophilia: Avant-Garde Paris and Black Culture in the 1920s.
66. Barthes, Roland Mythologies (1972), Hill and Wang: New York.
67. Friedmann, John (1986) The world city hypothesis in Development and Change Volume 17, Issue 1, pages 69-83, January 1986.

NHA event in Paris (2014). Picture by C. Kedi

No local or Black French hairdressers or hair specialists were invited to share geographically and culturally targeted conversations. When questioned about the reasons why local Black hair experts were not considered, the answer was that Afro-Americans tend to attract more publicity in the Black French and Parisian on/offline natural hair industry. (see next picture, C. Kedi 2014).

SALLE C

10H30
CLARISSE LIBENE
JANE CARTER

11H45
LES SOEURS MONROE

16H45
CLARISSE LIBENE
JANE CARTER

18H00
LES SOEURS MONROE

NHA event in Paris (2014). Picture by C. Kedi

LE CARREFOUR EUROPÉEN
DE LA BEAUTÉ ET DES TALENTS AFRO

1ᴱᴿ, 2 & 3 JUIN 2013
Palais des Congrès Paris-Est-Montreuil

SALON BOUCLES D'EBENE

Boucle d'Ebène event in Paris (2013). Courtesy of Boucle d'Ebène

The picture above is related to Boucle d'Ebene (created in 2005) features the first Salon dedicated to African hair type in its natural form where local experts were invited along with Europe-based and US-based specialists in African hair.

Two main approaches have been observed in Black communities living in "Latin" speaking countries/cultures: *mestizaje* and *négritude*[68]. *Mestizaje* refers to Black culture as being a mixture of European, Native American and African elements as part of the African experience in the Americas. One of its key leaders is the Afro-Cuban cultural activist, poet and intellectual, Nicolas Guillen (1902-1989). The other movement, *négritude*, is about the African element itself as a unique source of Black culture in Americas, the leading figure

---

68. Aime Cesaire (Mai-Juin 1935) numéro 3 de L'Étudiant Noir, Journal Mensuel de l'Association des Étudiants Martiniquais en France.

of that movement, apart from Senghor, was the Martinquan Aimé Césaire (1913-2008). Later, substitute African-orientated cultures appeared. They emerged following the disruption of the traditional way in which customs and social codes had always been passed down to the next generation. Finding themselves in a new and unfriendly environment they had difficulty in adjusting and in gaining the new social skills required. Not knowing much about their original nations (most of the slaves were kidnapped between the ages of 10 and 25), these Africans were unable to retain their culture after arriving in the Americas.[69] They were forced to adopt the dominating influences in America. Consequently, the African fashion space and beauty norms have been distorted from an African reality to create what we would call the birth of an African-American expression of beauty. With African imagery and as a consequence of an experience which they never asked for, the African-American notion of body adornment was shaped with a White-American angle. In addition given the world-wide influence of the American media, African-American beauty has become universal through PR and advertising, using pictures of much-admired and westernized beauties such as Hattie Mac Daniel (1895-1952) or Diana Ross (1944-).

In the French speaking countries of Africa and in most parts of the continent, dressing the body may defer more to religious beliefs or influences, as mentioned by Berenice Geoffroy-Schneider[70]. People did not have access to a variety of local or foreign cultures. The imitation of "exotic" European dressing codes was often not based on personal and community knowledge and tradition about clothing the body. This approach could have succeeded if the typical African on the street was familiar with the history of African fashion. The way in which fashion is presented worldwide is out of context to non-western societies. For example, people in Africa have long ago started wearing coats and winter clothes to display their Westerniza-tion[71]. Local cultures of adorning the body have been contested and

69. Courtin, Philip De Armind (1969) The Atlantic Slave Trade: A Census.
70. Geoffroy-Schneiter, Berenice (2006) Africa Is in Style.
71. Geoffroy-Schneiter, Berenice (2006) Africa Is in Style.

finally disregarded by many today. Schools of traditional design of clothes have been repudiated as non-academic leading to the spread of fashion designs from the Middle East, America and Europe.

This Americanisation of Black cultures in Europe can be exemplified by the *Sapologie* movement in Paris and Brussels[72]. We will focus here on the Parisian experience. Recently, during a conference[73] at the Institut Français de la Mode, Muller described the obsession with the Parisian female look as: "The Parisian woman's excellence lies in her elegance, her attitude, her superiority in comparison to other women who might live in London, New York or St. Petersburg. It is due to her knowledge and her know-how in styling clothes". The fame of the French capital as first fashion city of Haute Couture has spread worldwide. The muses responsible for the distribution of that myth are fashion icons such as Kate Moss who is highly praised in France for her Parisian touch. Because of the Parisian propensity to globalise, the Parisian touch is international: Africans can claim it. According to Berenice Geoffroy-Schneider[74], the *Sapologie* movement was born during the era of rumba in the late 60s in both Congo-Brazzaville and Zaire (now Democratic Republic of Congo) as a response to the return of European-educated Africans to newly emancipated Africa. Modernity in Kinshasa at the time meant a Western lifestyle. This mentality has now dominated the entire continent. Captured by Angolan photographer Jean Depara (1928-1997), Americanization mirrored the Harlem Renaissance imagery and US Western movies of the time. The movement eventually developed and influenced the dress of a majority of people. This trend of wearing expensive Western fashion designers led to the development of the *Societe des ambianceurs et personnes elegantes,* an association supporting and regulating the African dandys, known as *sapeurs.* The rules of elegance were communicated through these networks promoting the cult of lavishness but

---

72. Gentlemen of Bacongo (2009) by Paul Goodwin.
73. La Parisienne: une figure de mode by Florence Muller, Institut Francais de la Mode on 4th September 2014: http://plus.franceculture.fr/la-parisienne-une-figure-de-mode
74. Africa Is in Style (2006) Geoffroy-Schneiter, Berenice.

neglecting African designers. Among these instructions, as notified by Berenice Geoffroy-Schneider[75]: "[…] to wear the latest from Paris and Italy, but make it African […]". Paris was also home of the expansion of African fashion through the eyes of photographers of the early years of the independence including Seydou Keita (1921-2001) and Johnson Donatus Aihumekeokhai Ojeikere (1930-2014). How many African designers have become mainstream leaders without a formal training or apprenticeship in European companies? Well-known Africans including Alphadi (1957-) and Alaïa (1940-) long ago joined the elite circles of the predominantly European dressing scene confirming the steps to follow to reach a global market. In this context of a tradition of sophistication among Black French, it can be expected that fashion trend setters of the 21st century will build on this legacy.

4. Germany: Afro-Germanity

According to Archer-Straw,[76] "images of Black people in European popular culture at the end of the nineteenth century conformed to the perceptions of those who depicted them […]. These perceptions were based on only cursory knowledge because of the limited interaction between Europeans and Africans." The historical presence of Black Christians in Europe can be noticed with the celebration of Saint Maurice[77] on 22nd September in the Roman Catholic Church, on 5th October in the African Coptic Church and on 27th December among the Orthodox Christians. This character was canonized following the Christian tradition of honouring people who were known for their positive actions in the communities they lived in as well as the "miracles" they supposedly performed while alive. Saint Maurice was one of those rare Christians to have left a good reputation as a Black person in Germany.

75. Africa Is in Style (2006) Geoffroy-Schneiter, Berenice.
76. Archer-Straw, Petrine (2000) Negrophilia: Avant-Garde Paris and Black Culture in the 1920s.
77. Also known as Mauritius, Moritz or Morris.

The Berlin Conference of 1884, the racial theories current in the late 19th century and finally the rise of Nazism in the Third Reich unfortunately undermined the beneficial image that Black people could have had in Germany. Nowadays, the presence of Blacks in Germany is often linked to colonial relationships. An historical introduction to the Black presence in Germany would help us understand the advancement of Black Europeans[78]. It would also provide useful background information for bloggers. We will focus on the 20th century. The modern mixed-race Afro-Germans[79] were the children of relationships between Black French or Black Americans or Africans (mainly from French colonies in West Africa) and German women during the First World War and they were persecuted. Some of them were integrated to the German society before and during the Third Reich as testified by Hans Massaquoi (1926-2013) in his autobiography.[80] Culturally diverse, the 800,000 Afro-Germans (in 2011)[81], of whom many are African-Americans alongside an older generation of Africans from the former German colonies – German East Africa (contemporary Burundi, Rwanda and mainland Tanzania); South-West Africa (modern Namibia); Cameroon and Togo. Namibia was the scene of the first genocide of the 20th century when the Herero and Nama people were massacred (1904-1907)[82]. Namibian Black German[83] is a pidgin language spoken by a minority of Namibians who in years returned to their country after 1990. What is interesting is that a few vlogs (video and blogs together) use this as a language

78. Black Star, The African Presence in Early Europe. Runoko Rashidi. Books of Africa (2011).

79. Massaquoi, Hans (1999) Destined to Witness: Growing Up Black in Nazi Germany.

80. Massaquoi, Hans (1999) Destined to Witness: Growing Up Black in Nazi Germany.

81. Mazon, Patricia (2005). Not So Plain as Black and White: Afro-German Culture and History, 1890-2000. Rochester: University of Rochester Press. pp. 2–3.

82. Whitaker Report by United Nations (1985).

83. Ana Deumerta, *Namibian Kiche Duits: The Making (and Decline) of a Neo-African Language,*University of Cape Town: http://www.mashpedia.com/Namibian_Black_German

of communication. Most of the recent Black immigrants to Germany are Nigerians, Cape Verdeans and Ghanaians.

The development of fashion cities has given birth to another phenomenon in migration: Black Americans moving to settle in Northern Europe and specifically Germany. The Afro-German blogosphere is equally represented by both Afro-Germans and other Blacks who decided to set up in the Germany. To clarify why some Africans and Black Americans are still choosing Germany as a primary destination when considering a migration in Western Europe, it would be interesting to analyse how German towns and cities have developed.

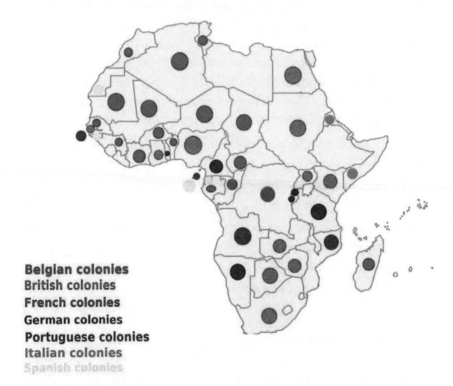

Belgian colonies
British colonies
French colonies
German colonies
Portuguese colonies
Italian colonies
Spanish colonies

African map of colonized lands circa 1902 adapted from Roland Oliver[84]

The separation of the two parts of Germany for almost 50 years created an unusual situation. The fall of the Berlin wall in 1989 led

---

84. The African experience (1991,1999) by Roland Oliver, p. 210.

to the introduction of globalization tothe German landscape through the expansion of Berlin as a dual city or divided city[85]. The economic focus in the reunited Germany attracted wealthy West Germans to invest and relocate to historical parts of former East Germany. Their lifestyles enabled the recruitment of lower income workers to work in their businesses or homes or to join the commercial restructuring of the area. A perfect example is the gentrified part of Berlin that will be descried in the next chapter. Furthermore, understanding the varied origins of the Afro-German communities highlights the differences in experiencing the local culture and relationships with indigenous people. As the most cosmopolitan city in Germany, Berlin is one of the most populated towns with a significant mix of various Black communities. Contemporary Berlin is known to have a vibrant cultural life, thus gaining recognition in the fashion world through the recent development of Berlin Fashion Week. The city has therefore attracted many Afro-Americans and Black British to establish themselves there alongside the significant German-born Black community (about 70 000)[86].

The Black blogosphere in Germany is therefore split into three main areas:

• The Afro-Germans blogging about lifestyle choices and local politics and integration.

• The expatriate Afro-Americans and British experiencing continental Europe and Germany.

• The second than third generation of German-born Africans connecting with Afropolitanism in European Union.

5. Portugal: Crioulos

The colonial relationship between Portugal and Africa started officially in 1415 when Ceuta in North Africa was captured. Portugal went on to colonise Brazil and to create bases along the coast of Africa. Brazil developed sugar plantations from the late 16th century

---

85. Urban geography by Kaplan, wheeler and Holloway (2009) p. 204-209.
86. http://isdonline.de/

and used human trafficking to cope with its rapid development. Portugal became one of the most powerful colonial states due to its capacity to import and export both men and sugar. Oliver and Atmore[87] highlight the methodology used in what became Angola to capture Africans for the transatlantic slave trade: "the strategy was to conquer first one and then another of the small *Mbundu* chieftainships, forcing the local rulers (called *sobas*) into a state of allegiance. The island of Sao Tome became the place where very large sugar plantations could be developed, each hosting up to 150 slaves[88]. Their testimonies were passed down to the next generation and the colonial power grew stronger by keeping local social groups such as the *Jaga* and *Yaka* people divided. For nearly 400 years, the Portuguese never truly culturally colonized the indigenous populations except on the coastal fringes. The Angola and Kongo cultures were affected by social challenges as they were taken as slaves to Brazil. This history explains the growth of a caste system based on skin colour. Still in contemporary Angolan, Congolese and Brazilian societies, the darker the skin complexion, the less the individual will be respected or acknowledged. This trend has unfortunately left some imprint on the Black Portuguese-speaking blogosphere which has generally chosen to display a faithful attitude to the skin codes. From the late 1600s, Fausto[89] explains that the colonial Brazilian society was distinguishing the slaves according to:

- their place of birth
- their skin colour
- their level of Portuguese
- their skills

In Brazil as in Black Caribbean, a racial caste system was institutionalised. Recently brought from Africa, slaves were named *Bocais* (singular *bocal*). The ones who were fluent in Portuguese and familiar

---

87. Oliver, Roland and Atmore Anthony (1967) Africa since 1800.
88. Medieval Africa 1250-1800, (2001) p. 171-179.
89. A concise history of Brazil (1999) by Boris Fausto. P. 24-28.

with colonial society were called *Ladinos*. Born in Brazil, they were identified as *Crioulos*. *Mulattos* were mixed-raced people born from a Portuguese parent and an African one. *Mamelucos* were children of native Indians and Portuguese. *Caboclos* or *Curibocas* were considered as nearly European as they had mainly Portuguese ancestry. *Cafusos* were born from a native Indian parent and an African one.

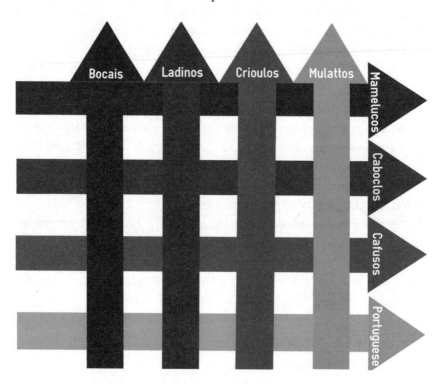

According to Malaquias[90] pre-colonial Angola up to the 15th century was populated by both large organised societies including the three main ones. These are still today the *Bakongo* (common to Angola and both modern Congos) representing about 15%; the *Ovimbundu* at 35 to 40% of the total population, the largest group; and the *Mbundu* also known as *Luandas* (as their original land was around the capital Luanda), representing 25% of the people. Angola was never

90. Ethinicity and conflict in Angola: prospects for reconciliation (2000) by Dr Assis Malaquias, p. 96-104.

fully united against the Portuguese colonization process since all the different people did not unify efficiently due to cultural and historical differences. As a matter of fact three different groups were launched to fight against the Portuguese during the decolonization process. We will focus here in the post-independence governing party which has heavily influenced contemporary Angolan society until now, the *Movimento Popular de Libertação de Angola* (MPLA), originally socialist and supported by the *Mbundu* as well as most *assimilados*, *mulattos* (one Portuguese parent and one African parent) and some Portuguese settlers. Being an *assimilado* meant being civilized and assimilated to Portuguese culture. This special status was proclaimed and developed in the legal text called the *Acto Colonial* (1930)[91].

Education, religion and lifestyles were used to transform Africans into assimilated "Europeans". Surnames were changed: almost all have names that are completely Portuguese.

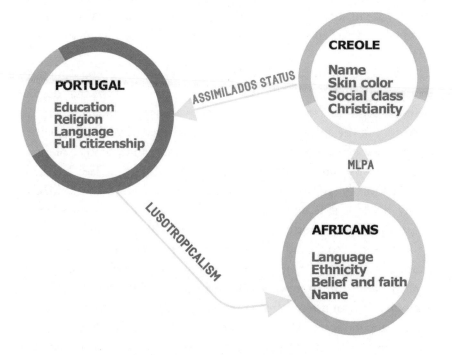

---

91. Living with Ambiguity, Integrating an African Elite in French and Portuguese Africa, 1930-61, Keese, Alexander (2006).

In that climate, being perceived as assimilated became the norm enabling the rise of a racialized colonial Angolan society. As an offspring of the Brazilian one, Angolan society inherited prejudices against African cultures and Black people's identities. The blogosphere in Portugal or Black Portuguese speaking countries still carries the heritage of what image of self can be presented to please the readership.

Conclusion

It seems that Africans" knowledge about self is likely to be affected by the history of colonial relationships. This has an impact on the promotion of African imagery and fashion – and therefore the Afropolitan expression of it. To allow an effective contribution to the global history of beauty and fashion as arts, Africans, their diaspora and other cultures should consider all the ways of acknowledging the original body in all societies, cultures, geographies and media.

Consequently, to assess the leading Black fashion blogosphere in France and elsewhere in Europe, it may mean to accept that despite a few exceptions (see last chapter), most blogging practitioners are accelerating the cultural denial of appreciating African bodies as they originally looked. The hypothesis of a hierarchy in the choice of dissemination of trends is one aspect of the blogging practice. Too little information is spread about African icons including Black African icons, Black Arab icons or even Black Caribbean icons in the fashion, lifestyle or beauty industries. I believe the Black fashion blogging sphere is eager to spread fashion using a largely Americanised iconography. Whether the motivations are due to lack of information about what is going on somewhere else (outside the Western world) or a supposed lack of interest from their readership, these bloggers may be acting unconsciously. They probably assume that their views on self are totally personal and genuine therefore they may not realise that presenting an American movie star as an ideal beauty on a blog (free platform online) can only intensify the US influence on the entire

Black community. As earlier mentioned, the Americanization of Black cultures worldwide (from Brazil to Portugal and elsewhere) using media domination as a marketing strategy to trade cosmetics, beauty ideals and practices has led to the reinforcement of painful habits such as valuing only USA-grown black beauties and ideals of beauty. The factors influencing the mechanisms of such customs are accentuated by racial prejudice. Fanon in his book the Wretched of the Earth (1961) mentioned:" [...] the oppressed will always believe the worst about them [...]". Therefore they could be summarized as:

- A destruction of collective identity
- A shift in cultural memory or ignorance of original cultures
- An assimilation of external values from winning model
- An internalization of foreign lifestyles
- Challenging own identities perceived as vanquished societies
- Desire to get closer to the domination/winning model.

With an introductive overview of in that prospect, the choice of location to launch online platforms will inform why European fashion cities give voices to citizen journalists.

Chapter II
Black europeans move up the social scale

1. Between cities

Bloggers have clearly been identified by the fashion industry as part of the process of dissemination of fashion using Internet exploration[92]. They are often described as writers of: "online diaries [...]"[93] who choose to escape the temporality of location and date."[94] Nevertheless, famous bloggers admit that in the beginning, when not always located in one of the fashion cities, they have had to hide the place (town, city or capital) where they were living if it was not one of them.[95] To evaluate how and why living in a global city may affect the success of an online platform targeted world cities are defined as "places where [...] corporations locate their management headquarters"[96]. Because of the presence of multinationals in a city, financial services, and other tertiary service providers concentrate in the area. Mainly located in the northern hemisphere, a hierarchy is applied according to several factors including the status of city as an international, regional or local centre[97]. The level of capitalist activity is a second important feature. The leading cities in the developing world can also be added to the list.

---

92. Rocamora, Agnès (2009) Fashioning the City: Paris, Fashion and the Media.
93. The cult of the amateur by Andrew Keen (2007).
94. The cult of the amateur by Andrew Keen (2007).
95. Discourse of blogs and wikis by Greg Myers (2009).
96. Urban Geography, 2nd edition (2009) by Kaplan, Wheeler and Holloway. P. 89.
97. The world city hypothesis (1986) by John Friedman.

Primary cities
Secondary cities

European world cities according to Friedmann in 1986

According to Friedmann (1986), there are two groups of world cities: the first are cities in the "core countries": a group of nations with a highly industrialized capacity, the leaders. This group includes: Chicago, New York and Los Angeles in the USA; Frankfurt in Germany; London in the United Kingdom; Rotterdam in the Netherlands; Paris in France; Zurich in Switzerland and Tokyo in Japan. The second group is made up of cities in industrialised countries with high numbers of corporations and capitalist activities but still not as developed as the core world cities: Brussels in Belgium; Madrid in Spain; Vienna in Austria; Houston, Miami and San Francisco in the USA; Sydney in Australia; and Toronto in Canada. The second set of world cities is in the "semi-peripheral countries". This group is also divided into primary and secondary cities. The first include Sao Paulo in Brazil and Singapore while in the secondary group of that section we find cities in Asia such as Bangkok, Hong Kong, Manila, Seoul and Taipei. Central and South America are represented by Buenos Aires. Caracas, Mexico City and Rio de Janeiro.

For the African continent, at the time only one city qualified as a world city: Johannesburg. Since the theory came out, numerous countries in Latin America and Asia have joined the higher ranks and no African cities have joined the network. The main reason being that less than 10 headquarters of multinationals are found in any African city. While London is the first European world city after New York and Tokyo, Milan and Paris are respectively in the 6th and 7th position[98]. As a matter of fact, similarly to the hierarchy of influence among Black communities around the world, choosing to settle in cities and capitals is still perceived as a criterion of success. Space allocation online seems to follow geography: dressing bodies in Milan is far more eclectic than shopping in a remote place in Italy. Living in Lisbon offers more attraction than inhabiting a town far from the ocean.

Afropolitans and subsequently bloggers have mainly common reasons for showcasing the different activities one place may offer: embellishment. To maintain a valuable and accurate number of followers, access to events, shopping centres, entertainment and the latest commercial products is vital. These actions have two functions: to create realism in the regular posts set by bloggers: talking about American celebrities when we are living in Europe would be in direct competition to gossip publications lacking means and networks. The costing of regular selfies around fashion capitals would emphasize the advantage that the blogger may have to offer in comparison to a trained journalist. In other words, embellishing private lives by mentioning places visited throughout the day, week or month is a social marker. This is to inform readers that the writer is "like them", meaning not an information professional but that the blogger is also a city citizen, a trendy person who obviously lives in a big city or a fashion capital. Barthes[99] analyses the birth of "the detail" in dressing bodies in France after the revolution. He explains that upper classes and especially the aristocracy had to maintain a class differentiation in

---

98. Source: Godfrey and Zhou, 1999, p. 276.
99. The Language of Fashion (2013) translated and printed by Bloomberg publications, p. 73.

clothing. To highlight the superiority in status: "A distinguished man is a man who marks himself off the crowd using modest means [...]". Fashion is a crowd phenomenon which can be judged in two ways: "according to the project itself" or "according to how the project has been carried out"[100]. In our evaluation of black blogs around fashion capitals in Europe we focused on how the project was carried out, noticing the cultural and local differences in each category of blog: fashion, beauty, lifestyle or general interest. Therefore the blogs we have approached are all based in European capitals or big cities and we can see now that being a capital or a big city does not automatically confer the title of "global city". This is also one of the numerous myths giving the illusion that capitals are better off in terms of job prospects: in reality they tend to be rich in cultural and historical symbolism but not necessarily economic worth.

2. Brussels and Geneva

In Belgium the black blogosphere has recently taken off, starting in the Belgian capital where a solid African community has been historically linked to the country since colonial times. Why focus on Brussels? This is because most of the African community there originates from the Democratic Republic of Congo as well as Rwanda and Burundi. Due to the use of two languages, French and Dutch (Flemish) in Belgium, the Black community there is aware of the linguistic prejudices of some Francophones trying to reach the Black Dutch-speaking community. It is also important to remember that the first three cotton mills which pioneered the wearing of wax prints in Africa, were established in the 1830s in Haarlem in the Netherlands. They created the *Dutch Trade Company.*[101] Dutch entrepreneurs were finding ways to commercialise competitively priced Asian batiks to Africans to clothe their naked bodies. "African" wax prints have numerous names including *Superwax*, *Wax blocks* and *Real*

---

100. The Language of Fashion (2013), translated and published by Bloomsbury, Roland Barthes, p. 75.
101. Fashion the whole story by Marnie Fogg and Valerie Steele (2013) p. 160-163.

Dutch Wax. The link with the Brussels blogosphere is that some of the earliest African people to have worn these Dutch wax prints were some of the Congolese. There may be links between the *Sapologie* movement (keen interest in wearing European-types of fine clothing) with the emergence of *"Dutch Wax"*. Nevertheless, two main online platforms including a magazine and a blog have increased the online influence of this part of the African diaspora in Europe.

Two examples of Afro-Belgian blogs

Both written in French, the successful Black Belgian blogosphere is influenced by the European culture in which it communicates. French is spoken in 57 countries in the world and 220 million speakers use it as a first language;[102] 20 other countries study it as a second language. The use of French is promoted by the *Organisation Internationale de la Francophonie (OIF)*. *Francophonie* can be described as the entire community of people and countries who speak French. The word

---

102. Source: Organisation Mondiale de la Francophonie (2010) available from: http://www.francophonie.org/

was used for the first time in 1880[103] by geographer Onésime Reclus (1837-1916) who was a specialist in France and its relationship with its colonies. With 30 African countries as members or associates, the OIF aims at maintaining the diffusion of French language and its culture through learning and practice and through diplomacy.

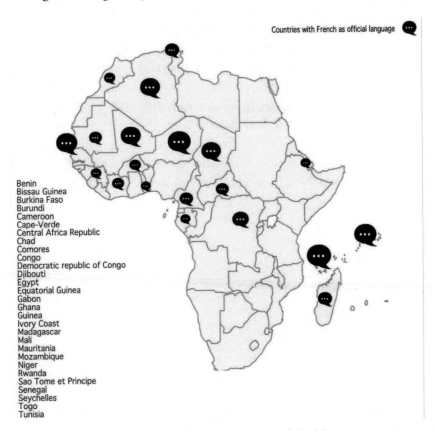

Benin
Bissau Guinea
Burkina Faso
Burundi
Cameroon
Cape-Verde
Central Africa Republic
Chad
Comores
Congo
Democratic republic of Congo
Djibouti
Egypt
Equatorial Guinea
Gabon
Ghana
Guinea
Ivory Coast
Madagascar
Mali
Mauritania
Mozambique
Niger
Rwanda
Sao Tome et Principe
Senegal
Seychelles
Togo
Tunisia

African countries which are members of the OIF

Since ex-Belgian colonies inherited the French language as their first European language of communication, it is natural that the most-followed Black blogs in Brussels are written in French. To evaluate the role of a language as a code of communication when addressing

---

103. http://www.francophonie.org/

specific targeted group of people, Bignell[104] explains that semiotics (also known as semiology): "is the study of signs in society, and while the study of linguistic signs is one branch of it". He later states that as the most persuasive and basic form of human interaction, language inspires other types of semiotics. This is where culture and society establish the meaning of each word, linking them to a concept. Bignell defends the opinion that: "All of our thought and experience, our very sense of our own identity, depends on the systems of signs already existing in society which give form and meaning to consciousness and reality". The organisations of all the systems used to communicate (including words, images, clothing or food) are named "codes". For blogs and bloggers, it is likely that they have chosen the type of imagery and words to exchange specific information, even if they usually imply that they write with spontaneity. "Signifiers" are sounds, alphabetical letters and photos. "Signifieds" are words and concepts allocated to them.

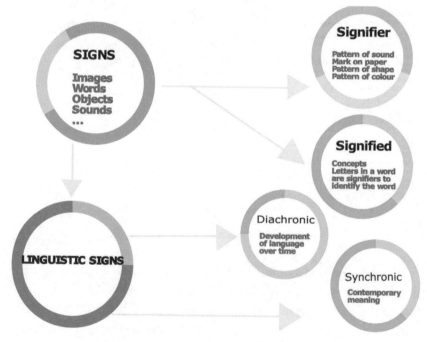

Components of the sign section (sources: Bignell, Saussure)

104. Media semiotics an introduction, p. 1-12.

In other words, we can only shape meanings or visualize concepts based on codes agreed according to linguistic signs. These semiotics may refer to the development of a language over a certain period of time. In this case, they are called *diachronic* linguistic signs. Or these signs can be the mirror of contemporary meanings and they would be named *synchronic* linguistic signs. When now considering the Black Belgian blogosphere, we are dealing with people who are influenced by the l Belgian version of French combined with the Black African experience of French inherited through relatives often born in Africa. The French spoken within France itself is varied in expression, tone, accent and meaning. Academic French also has different characteristics. The French spoken in Brussels, Kinshasa or Algiers has adapted to its environment. Now, after several migrations of people, diachronic linguistic signs for the French language spoken in different parts of the world by various ethnic groups may transform words to make sense within a specific context. A good example is the word *rendez-vous*. The synchronic linguistic sign when using this word in English means "a date". In French, the exact same word means *"an appointment"*. Another example in the Black community would be the use of the word *"brune"*. For Africans originating from Central Africa this word means "a light skinned woman". For French speakers in the Western world, the same word means a "dark haired woman" *brunette* in English.

Due to the impact of meanings within cultural contexts, we can confirm that a blog written by Black people living in Brussels for instance will reflect the local feel and lifestyle. That blog will primarily attract a mirroring readership despite being online. The reason for this is that to locate a blog, according to Myers,[105] is not really possible as the very nature of it is to be "placeless" as Internet can be accessed regardless of space and time. However, he indicates that locating a blog can only be done by identifying where the equipment allowing the blogging to happen (computers, mobile devices) is based. This analysis is applicable to the Western type of blogs.

105. Discourse of blogs and wikis by Greg Myers (2009) p. 48-49.

When dealing with the Black blogosphere, I would take a different approach. Community-based with both entertaining and informative agendas, Black blogs cater for Black online communities by specifically dealing with subjects affecting them. Successful bloggers are those who exploit anonymity to enhance social interactions. As Myers recalls: "The internet breaks down the boundary between the experts and the novices, so anyone can contribute."[106]

Brussels, now the capital of the European Union has a long history. The city was founded in 979.[107] The Ixelles quarter of Brussels where most Blacks are located is known as *"Matonge-Ixelles."*[108]. Thename came from a popular red fruit which was found in the *Kasa-Vubu* quarter in the Congolese capital, Kinshasa. In time *Kasa-Vubu,* also knolwn as Matonge, became the most crowded and lively area of Kinshasa which led to the Ixelles quarter of Brussels being dubbed Matonge.[109] Congolese students were housed in this part of town and the Democratic Republic of Congo had its embassy nearby. Naturally the Congolese community started gathering in the area, developing food and culturally-focused businesses.

According to the local authorities, *Matonge-Ixelles* is an ethnic-oriented market and business area, hardly a place to live for most Africans. The social positioning of new African migrants and solidarity to newcomers is important for the community circulating there. Brussels for bloggers is therefore a cosmopolitan location, an entertaining area easy to access, a convenient place to meet with Blacks and Africans in general. It is important to notice that Black African immigration in Belgium was never encouraged by the colonial government. They favoured Italian, Turkish, Moroccan and Spanish immigrants. Congolese people migrated on their own. This may explain the reason why the two successful blogs we investigated in Brussels shared certain views on social media about local and daily

---

106. Discourse of blogs and wikis by Myers, Greg (2009) p. 22.
107. Source: official website for Brussels city: www.brussels.be.
108. Source: http://www.questionsante.org/bs/Matonge-Ixelles
109. Source: Sociologie du quartier Matonge, Un coin d'Afrique à Ixelles, étude de l'asbl Reform, Décembre 1997.

challenges met by Black people. With a blog targeting mainly women but also men, there are discussions and updates about the social moves within the community which have nourished an Afro-Belgian culture of reference to Brussels as the contact point for any Black person living there. The two bloggers we interviewed set up their online platforms in late 2011. That year was a particular success in the beauty and fashion blogosphere since the Black European online world witnessed the transformation of a popular webzine into a printed magazine after three years of intense activity.

The Paris-based self-proclaimed "high quality" publication organised set a crowd-funding campaign online to make their dream come true. Initiated by four young Black Parisians, the blog wanted to feature iconic images and positive photographs of Blacks wearing trendy outfits. The success was immediate due to the quality of the images and the targeted market which at the time was mainly the 18-25 age group. The dominance of Paris was also reflected in the publication: only Black US and Black French celebrities were initially featured, preferring to display a "Black French" identity rather than an African one. Blacks were, and still are, featured as socially assimilated. In fact Black French-speaking Europe saw an increase in online publications, notably beauty online diaries.

The owners of both online platforms' based in Brussels have family roots in the Democratic Republic of Congo. An important identity element as we will see later is that not all Black bloggers associate themselves with non-European areas as their countries of origin. I asked the two bloggers what would best describe the purpose of their online platform: is it for beauty, fashion, lifestyle, art or all of the above. They both answered "all of the above." Probably due to the small size of both Belgium and Brussels limits the size of the Black Belgian community, creating a specialized online publication would have been risky as the readership would be small. Both answered that "open-minded" would be one of the adjectives which would best describe themselves and their online platforms. Their images reflect the social advancement of Black Europeans, social differences, cultural events and entertainment likely to appeal to this group.

An event set up by the association managing the online platform "Just Follow Me"

A beauty related event organised by both Just Follow Me and Sista Diaspora

The two locations chosen to initiate the meeting of these two blogs' followers were both located in socio-economically parts of the trendy Brussels. The *Bourgeois-Bohème*[110] (commonly known as BOBO) movement was officially qualified for the first time by American Brooks[111]. His theory was (and still is) being debated since it acknowledged what was already going on in Greenwich Village, New York in the mid to late 1990s. Some commentators have identified sub-groups including "creative", "hipsters" and others. The "creatives" would be the generation of people primarily associated with their jobs, lifestyle and skills rather than their wealth. Richard Florida, urbanist and academic, has created a website dedicated to the understanding of this "middle class".[112] The "hipsters" would be distinguished by their lower income. Both would be slightly less influential than the BOBO.[113] Nowadays, this lifestyle, as predicted by Brooks, has conquered Europe. Seldom used to describe people other than Europeans, the BOBO possesses its own icons and key people or trend setters depending on the context and country. The BOBO lifestyle is mainly presented by Western media as a lifestyle option. Because of the tendency of "Black Europeans" to absorb what is culturally dominant in any country they live in, the need to re-create an "Afro" version of BOBOs had to occur. The Europe-based Black blogosphere certainly tends to identify with this bohemian depiction of self: creatives in their choice of careers, excellent in their communication strategies and brilliant in visual stimulation, the Black version of BOBOs is real. To the following question: are they "Black" BOBOs? The answer is yes, the equivalent exists in Black cultures, the Afropolitans or the "Afropolitan tribe"! This trend has led to the gentrification of traditionally popular areas.

---

110. Bobos In Paradise: The New Upper Class and How They Got There by David Brooks (2000).
111. The writer proposed a thesis about an upcoming upper class ritualized around a lifestyle inherited from the hippies while having an entrepreneurial and capitalist wallet.
112. Source: http://www.creativeclass.com/richard_florida
113. Source: Plevin, Julia (2008-08-08). "Who's a Hipster?", www.huffingtonpost.com

There is an equivalent trend affecting Black people in Brussels which has led to the gentrification of traditionally community areas. These two bloggers organised their event, *A Beauty Case,* in November 2013 at l'*Atelier des Tanneurs,* an improvised organic food store. As mentioned earlier, African migration to Belgium was voluntary: the first generations of Congolese who set up in Brussels were likely to have come from the wealthier class in Congo or from different backgrounds but keen to move up the social scale through education. These first migrants' children were raised in Brussels, creating an identity link with the city. Consequently, these second and third generations, if they pursue their families' ambitions to either maintain their social status or improve it, may have achieved their goals and acquired economic and social capital. This has allowed the emergence of a blogosphere willing to share views and values of being black in Brussels with like-minded people. The new Black "gentry" of Brussels comprises art-school trained professionals, business owners and various culturally aware individuals: together, they form an online presence. Finally, since the 90s Brussels has produced many fashion designers who now work in international fashion houses. The city has embraced this new online Black community quicker than in London, Paris or Berlin. The awareness of European trends has become characteristic of Brussels through the *Sapologie* movement. I will compare these findings with those in other fashion capitals, London, Paris and Berlin. Despite the similarities with Parisian bloggers for: the readership (mainly female), location of followers (mainly Brussels) and the number of hits on the website, the main differences in terms of market are orientated towards: different types of awareness strategies e.g. organisation of events; community orientated communication using social media and traditional media (radio, magazine and TV); and the closely connected network of Belgian bloggers who work together. This does not necessarily exist in London, Paris or Berlin.

The Geneva blogosphere is a consequence of the specific demography of the African community living in Switzerland. Most of the African and Caribbean people live in Geneva and the blogs are concentrated in the city which is a favourite location for migrants. Geneva also hosts many United Nations agencies and is home to an international crowd of bankers, diplomats, civil servants and well-off citizens of the world, some of whom are Africans. Online Swiss-based Afropolitans are is interested in politics and culture and in connecting with the global blogosphere. The needs of the local readership are shaped and influenced by the complicated social conditions of the Black community. During the second period of Black migration into Switzerland, particularly Geneva, from the mid-90s onwards, the motives were economic and they aimed at assimilation but they did not all reach Geneva for the same purpose. According to the African Council in Switzerland,[114] around 60,000 Africans live in the country and they are live in the 26 cantons that form the Republic.[115] The largest groups of Black Africans are: Eritreans: 7,370, Somalis: 6,400, Congolese (DRC): 5,845, Angolans: 4,365 and Cameroonians: 4,340. With the large African community in Geneva, the Black blogs in Switzerland offer many types of communication tools, strategies and contents. One of the websites is managed by a middle-aged man while another belongs to a young woman. One is an online magazine while another is a webzine or vlog[116]. In both cases, they are Geneva-born and describe their origins as Congolese, trained in marketing and market research. Love and passion are also adjectives they used to describe their blogs or themselves. This could be interpreted as understanding the role of their respective online platforms as promoters of the active Black community in Switzerland.

Mia-culture.com is an online magazine which used to be printed and translated from English to enable a majority of Africans to read it in French. Communication among Blacks in Geneva benefits from a dynamic academic scene. The existence of a "people's university" (*Universite Populaire Africaine* UPA.ch) reminds Africans that, despite

---

114. Source: http://www.africancouncil.ch/fr
115. Source: http://www.cipina.org/preacutesence-africaine-en-suisse.html The Black African community is distributed as follows: Geneva 26%, Vaud 20%, Zurich 13%, Berne 10%, Fribourg 5% and Neuchâtel: 5%.
116. video blog.

living in one of the wealthiest areas in Europe; without the discomfort of a colonial relationship with its inhabitants, the reason why they left their countries was still linked to the economy and politics, inherited from history. Geneva is also a totally francophone city, although German is the biggest of the four Swiss languages. Mia-culture.com is an online magazine which used to be printed and translated in English to enable a majority of Africans to read it in the French language. Mia-culture.com is a sign system which might either create concepts in terms of identity such as Afro-Swiss lexicology or cultural references only understandable by locals or to the contrary and which erases concepts which cannot be expressed due to cultural differences.

The main difference from Brussels is that events in Geneva are less entertaining in their nature and are focused around the diffusion of information. The main differences from cities such as London or Paris is the scale of the population to target. With the highest rate of diversity of African nationalities in Europe and a smaller community spread all over the country, the Swiss blogosphere faces multiple challenges: language, culture, networks. Reaching the non-French speaking Africans means possessing adequate networks and understanding their mode of communication. The other serious challenge the Swiss blogs may encounter is the "emergency factor". The Black community in that part of Europe is already exposed to press and media from all around the world as well as Black blogs in Europe, USA and Africa. To create a competitive edge for disseminating information, the Black blogs in Geneva are obliged to provide local news and features. This information is seldom covered by national or supranational networks as the market is considered to be "niche".

3. Paris and Lisbon

Christopher Breward [117] explains that: "'Paris fashion' […] represent[s] one of the most powerful and long-running reifications of place in modern history". From colonial times, the fascination

---

117. Fashion's World Cities (2006).

of Paris as the capital of fashion was long established in African and diaspora circles. As shown by Dr Agnes Rocamora[118] in her concept of a fashion city, a "Paris myth" has developed: "The centrality of Paris in all things cultural is consecrated, as it has been since the 17th century. The fashion city is a link between the city's history and the development of fashion there. Fashion cities have developed a culture of fashion as an ultimate sign of civilization and modernity, between arts and industry. The Parisian fashion scene reflects with accuracy the reason why some Black bloggers associate themselves with this city and not with an African fashion city such as Dakar. The fascination of Paris is also partly due to the fact that the city attracts all type of migrants who want to consume, sell, make and wear Parisian fashion. A long tradition of international talents celebrating the city for its fashion craftsmanship and creativity started officially with Charles Worth (1825-1895). Nationalities originating from the five continents have come together to create this Parisian look which is "[…] a matter of collective pride […]" as fashion "[…] involves a whole capital, […] through the capital, a whole nation […]."[119]

Among the few Paris-based bloggers interviewed, two were located in the centre of Paris having moved from other areas of the country as soon as opportunities arose. They would describe themselves without hesitation as *Parisienne* or *Africaine*, some tracing back their families to the continent, others being from the second, third or fourth generation of immigrants. Their personal choices and experiences have helped create the Black Parisians' identity in France. The assimilation of Black Europeans parallels the gentrification of inner cities and close suburbs. From the data obtained for the survey sent to the first 18 Black European bloggers, three were Paris-based and all were trained in either marketing, journalism or business studies with a propensity for their online platforms to offer services, specific data or the promotion of some locations within Paris and its surroundings. These blogs reflected the choice of studies by the community of African descent in France in general, the trend

---

118. Fashioning the city: Paris, fashion and the media (2009).
119. Fashion's World Cities (2006)

of creating one's own job since the early 1990's and the inspirational successes of Afro-Americans as entrepreneurs. The choice to study marketing, business studies or journalism is related to an industry in which market research and research skills are highly valued. Therefore the training is targeted at customer relations. Most of the leading Black French bloggers studied at business schools since universities were offering more academic and theoretical views on business. This choice is also the consequence of the local job market which favoured students who could afford private schools rather than public universities. Business schools also provide an opening to the corporate world largely dominated by American-type capitalism. Creating one's own activity is one of the things taught in many business schools. Therefore, after graduation, many Black French graduates choose to experiment with paid jobs before testing the entrepreneurship road. These last few years have seen many successes by young Black French entrepreneurs who have started businesses and expanded businesses, even global organisations. The culture of the creation of capital through self-employment is relatively valued and strong among the younger generation.

Belle Ebene
www.bellebene.com
Republic Democratic of Congo and Senegal
Lives in France
Launched in 2008
Few words: tips and sales of cosmetic products for dark and mixed raced skin tones

The cult of Oprah Winfrey as the ultimate mogul in a racially challenged society inspired others to try to emulate her. Our respondents have extensively travelled in at least three continents before reaching middle age and their studies, location and taste reflected a tendency to favour relaxation and quality time rather than economy. In France people who started their careers less than 20 years ago have been used to working fewer hours, balancing the private and public areas of their lives and aiming at higher paid jobs to acquire the resources for entertainment and leisure activities. Blacks are no exception to this. Their exposure to various cultures and environments can be perceived on their online platform and the way they choose to describe it. While some of the media tools for disseminating Afropolitan culture might require some complicated organisation to cover as many events as possible, the use of online platforms by inner-city inhabitants seems to have been a favourable factor in the expansion of the Parisian-based fashion and lifestyle blogosphere. Photojournalism is the preferred method of communication with a wider audience. The use of photography in these Black French blogs supports the idea of being a "high-profile fashion blog."[120] Following a rich tradition in photojournalism begun by Henri Cartier-Bresson (1908-2004) and Jacques Henri Lartigue (1894-1986), the Black French blogosphere is under pressure to portray Parisian lifestyle and the chic local fashion. This behaviour enriches a network of viewers: "New users [a]re attracted to sign up to the site. [...] Network effect is a driving force behind the [...] model."[121] Through the use of codes of identification including leisure time, language and geographical references (many of these blogs speak about streets or arrondissements, assuming that everyone knows it refers to Paris, these online trend setters acknowledge the proximity that the Internet and its virtual friendship and links may create. Not knowing each other personally, readers have shared interests which remain the same over long periods of time. This situation has consequences on a national scale: people see photographs of Paris or popular places in the city and

---

120. Fashion Blogs by Kirstin Hanssen, Felicia Nitzsche & Elina Tozzi p. 19.
121. Facebook, the future of its ad-supported business model by Marketline on January 2013. p. 9.

are inspired. The online community is made up of readers who can immediately identify with the bloggers and their lifestyle. They may be able to visit the places mentioned in the blog but if they do not live in the same city they may have perceptions about how glamorous life may be there. How difficult it might be to build visibility and credibility when blogging using images about anywhere but Paris!

Lisbon is to Portugal and its ex-colonies what London is to the Commonwealth, a place of historical migration of Africans. What is now Portugal was ruled by the Moors for nearly 800 years[122] and the term "Black Portuguese" is still a taboo. How many Blacks live in Lisbon is unclear since, official policy in Portugal does not allow the classification of Portuguese citizens by race.[123] As in France, the assimilation policy during colonial times left a bitter taste to non-indigenous Portuguese. Gilberto Freyre (1900-1987) developed the idea of Luso-tropicalism[124] which proudly assumed that Portuguese colonisers who intermarried with enslaved Africans and native Indians of Brazil could create a multi-racial Portuguese culture and society in Brazil and in Africa. Freyre declared that Portugal also had a natural ability and a winning approach to live peacefully with colonised indigenous people.[125]

122. The African Presence in Early Europe (2011) Runoko Rashidi.
123. The Guardian on 12th September 2011: http://www.theguardian.com/commentisfree/2011/sep/12/portugal-race
124. The Masters and the Slaves: a study in the development of Brazilian civilization (1933) by Gilberto Freyre.
125. Colorbling colonialism? (2007) thesis by Leah Fin. P. 10-22.

Lisbon is one of the oldest cities in Europe[126] with a long tradition of foreigners mixing with local people. Our investigation traced one Portuguese speaking blogger who is based in Switzerland. She agreed to take part in the study and could interact in either English or French. As her online platform is written in Portuguese, her readership is among Portuguese speakers wherever they may be located. Her readership is mainly located in Europe, in Luxembourg, Geneva and Lisbon. I questioned her about Afropolitans settling in Lisbon. It is a port and an administrative centre, a cosmopolitan city filled with tourists and entertainment. The large movement of African settlers to Portugal happened in the 1970s during and soon after the independence struggles in Angola, Cape Verde, Guinea Bissau, Mozambique and Sao Tome. The migrants were initially mainly men who started opening businesses in Largo de Sao Domingos, a quarter situated in the centre of Lisbon. This became something of a ghetto: loneliness developed. Wives and family left behind were reunited with their husbands and male family members in the 1980s. The economy was in crisis as the job market became increasingly harsh. The situation is similar today with the difference that large numbers of Black Portuguese have now started considering other parts of Europe or Africa to move to. Lisbon and Portugal cannot now cater for the growing numbers of people leaving Africa and pursuing economic stability in the colonial motherland. The fact that many Black Portuguese who may have been born and raised in Portugal now live elsewhere partly explains the nature of the Black Portuguese blogosphere. It is a meeting point for the *fashionistos* and *fashionistas* sharing language and codes such as interest in dances including *Kizomba, Kuduro* or *Semba*. The first fashion street style bloggers in Lisbon have emerged during dance festivals. While attending events, evening shows and nightclubs, they would eventually catch the latest from the dance floor. Fashion and style are promoted within these dancing circles: top choreographers, promoters, producers, entertainers, venue owners and Saturday night

---

126. Official Tourism office for Portugal: https://www.visitportugal.com/en/sobre-portugal/biportugal

crowds. A network of like-minded people. In Lisbon Afropolitans who still refer to Africa as their reference.

4. London and Berlin

Berlin is the historical capital of Germany, which, despite having had African colonies is still a challenging place to live for Black people. Of the two Black bloggers based in Germany who answered the questionnaire, neither were born German. One was living in Berlin and came from the USA and the other moved about three years ago to Dusseldorf with her existing fashion platform. Both said that Germany was different from an English speaking country in the sense that writing about local life for the African-American blogger became vital to share her views and daily challenges. Language, cultural references and environment were unfamiliar to her for a long period of time. The need to meet like-minded people became urgent. Both the bloggers have similarities: marketing trained them to understand their viewership and both share valuable information. One of the blogs is about ethical fashion within an African-orientated environment. Her successful platform generates thousands of hits per day and has won awards several times for both the quality of its content and for its design. The other is more of a traditional blog, the online diary of an expatriate American sharing with fellow Americans in and outside Germany her life in the city. Whilst our first blogger provides international information and does not indicate a specific place, the second is only focusing on Berlin. The city of Berlin has recently started to acknowledge African fashion during its fashion week.[127] Black bloggers in Germany thus have an event and a place to meet. They also have fashion content to disseminate locally and internationally. Both these blogs choose English as a language of dissemination in our two case studies is a consequence of them not being originally from that culture, but both where attracted to Berlin by the intense creative activities which have made it famous, including within

127. http://www.fashion-week-berlin.com/

the Afropolitan community. Berlin also has a larger proportion of old-established inhabitants which gives it an authenticity within the town that London and Paris have nearly lost. Afropolitans in Berlin and elsewhere often claim a double heritage: a Western citizenship coupled with an African identity. As a consequence, their awareness of both worlds helps sustain a lifestyle and interest in everything geographically, socio-economically and creatively in Europe, America and Africa. Blacks have different perceptions, experiences and realities in Berlin and therefore they feel the need to write about it. This is different from the Black Parisian blogger who writes because s/he has citizenship but also sometimes identity struggles. (German citizenship is not given so easily to those who are not German by descent.) Black bloggers in Germany are different from their counterparts in Lisbon: they are not assimilated and are noted more for their physical differences than their lifestyle choices.

London was the birthplace of the term "Afropolitan" (and "Afrpolitanism") as well as being the leading trend creator for the Afropolitan fashion scene. Over the last twelve years, the growing style of European-based African fashion has blossomed here due to a mixture of events, the launch of both online and offline boutiques, the promotion of designers by both African stylists and photographers and, of course, blogs. Afropolitan east Londoners such as the boutique *Soboye* in Shoreditch[128] were among the first trend setters in developing the idea of a fashion boutique with an exhibition type of display. Similarly, the *Larache* boutique of the renowned Moroccan photographer and artist Hassan Hajjaj[129] determinedly supported the idea that African identity is not limited to the place where people were born but certainly to their original culture – the culture they have inherited from their parents, the culture that shaped their forefathers' identity. In this analysis, out of four London-based bloggers at the time of the survey, three referred to themselves as being both anthropologically from UK and being citizens of UK. The two other bloggers, both born in Africa, associated themselves with

128. http://soboye.tictail.com/
129. http://www.taymourgrahne.com/artists/hassan-hajjaj

being Afropolitan on the basis of their place of birth. The question in my mind afterwards was: what about people born outside Africa to African parents? Are not they African too?

London is the most diverse city in Europe and possibly in the world in terms of ethnicity. It is in London where the most surprising answers came when asking questions about identity, citizenship and Afropolitanism. Black people in London feel culturally-mixed, not just culturally influenced and would describe themselves as "Afropean", "mixed", and "multicultural. This identity crisis has largely shaped the way Black bloggers in London present the city. London is described as a multi-ethnic city with varied ties to five continents, the stepping stone to the English-speaking African world. To the Afropolitan movement it is a compulsory first stop. Similarly, the two blogs run by creative professionals are those who described themselves as both "thoughtful" and "explorative". This lack of an answer to some of the following questions can encourage the readers to check online to see how they present their platform. With their profiles described as "social or "promoting sustainability", the collective approach to ethics using the online medium is in keeping for a country which houses some of the most famous charities in the world such as Oxfam and Save the Children. Afropolitan south Londoners also play an important role as trend creators and trend setters since they are found around Brixton where the historical Afro-Caribbean journey of the early 20th century started. Boutiques such as *Pempamsie,* established in 1997 on Brixton Hill, act as lifestyle and general interest stopovers where fashion and beauty are fundamentals.

Although London has had a small Black population in past centuries, the arrival of the first large number of immigrants from the Caribbean on the ship, the *Windrush* in 1948 was the start of a significant Black presence. The history of this presence has been preserved in the Black Cultural Archives whose permanent location was opened in July 2014 in Windrush Square, Brixton. Consequently, the Black blogosphere in the UK is one of the most diverse in Europe. Bloggers in different parts of the country cover subjects from ethical fashion, beauty and lifestyle to nude photography of black women, nutrition, decor and art. The versatility, knowledge, impact and dynamism of this most cosmopolitan city in the world can also be measured against the number of Black nationalities living in London. Many African ethnicities can be met in the capital making it a special place for cultural references, catering for people from all over the continent. Due to the relative concentration of Blacks in London in some areas (Brixton, Clapham, Croydon, Hackney, Lewisham, Peckham, Stratford, Tottenham, Wood Green) some local boroughs celebrate their diversity with culturally related activities such as festivals like Brixton Splash or during Black History Month; or in the names of locations such as the Marcus Garvey Library, the CLR James Library, the Olive Morris building; and in streets named after Nelson Mandela. However, this historical presence is not always well known among young people. Influenced by mainly Americanised media, young Black British seek quick and convenient ways to get information relevant to themselves that can be used on a daily basis.

In this climate, the Black British blogosphere in London has exploded. Offering shortcuts to books and magazines, easy-to-digest information is made up of images, American types of data including rarely broadcast news related to Black American celebrities on a daily basis. The challenge for the Black upmarket British bloggers is to avoid copying what Black Americans do online. With various origins, cultures and languages, living in Europe, with diverse goals (unlike the long history of Blacks in the USA) copying is definitely not the best option. Unfortunately, too often Rihanna, Béyoncé and others are gracing the pages of Black British online platforms in an attempt to attract viewership. After a few months or years of American entertainment news, eventually bloggers either make a living or leave the scene.

In this study, we have tried as much as possible to target and track bloggers who are not dependent on what is going on outside the place they live in. As opinion leaders or influencers, they need to be exposed to and to have experienced what is going on here and now. The list was reduced since the American inspiration is widely spread on online British platforms. I concentrated on blogs with a high percentage of local-based content for those who are willing to get simple and sourced information related to specific subjects. Mainly London based, our choice of leading Black bloggers in the UK supported our desire to also promote their specific priorities. From our investigation, out of 21 blogs, only 16,66% were of Caribbean descent. To conclude, catering for Black Europeans from a fashion perspective is about identifying who the key players are, where they create trends and why they are located in specific places in Europe, often matching the mainstream socio-geographical trends. The next section will introduce the understanding of how do they disseminate the trends and how effective their business strategies are.

In all these cities the Afropolitan crowd is made up of a mixture of long term immigrants who eventually chose to settle in Europe but who are still a minority added to the majority of more recent generations of African and Caribbean immigrants. Trend creation is born in Africa, appreciated and transformed in Brussels, London, Berlin and Lisbon usually with an American touch added – and finally the trend is disseminated back to Africa through the channel of fashion cities including Lagos, Nairobi, Dakar, Johannesburg, Abidjan, Marrakech or Luanda. Both the Europe-based and the Africa-based Afropolitans are influenced by the Afropolitans living in European fashion capitals. To the questions: what are they talking about? What do they spend their leisure time on? We might refer to conversations about food at the newest Afro restaurant in Brussels or Berlin. They might talk about the recent book or exhibition dedicated to recent African history. They might describe the latest concert of one of the most popular Afro stars (often American or European by citizenship rather than African). These Afropolitan trend setters may have an impact on city-type activities: shopping, travelling, going out, art, food and entertainment. In the next section we will evaluate the success of these bloggers. What is a successful Afropolitan blogger in Europe? Are they popular? If yes, how should we measure their popularity? Do social media support the definition of celebrity? What are the differences between popularity, celebrity and icon?

Part II

Black female bloggers and their interests

Chapter III
Black Beauty Blogs

1. Overview of the beauty industry

For an accurate understanding of the influence of Afropolitan bloggers on Black Europeans through social media, it should first be placed into a chronological frame. The second layer of investigation would be to understand the chronological place of Afro hair care mediatisation in a Western context. Then we can analyse modern strategies used by both bloggers and manufacturers to disseminate Afro hair care trends. The first black female blogs in Europe were about beauty, specifically hair. Following the growing trend of accepting natural African hair types without chemical treating, known widely as "relaxers" by Afro-Americans in the 1990s, some academic and Black activists started to question the validity of the Black woman's physical appearance initially in US society and by extension to the rest of the world. To cite a few of them I have chosen Juliette Smeralda from Martinique, Kobena Mercer from the UK and Ghana, and Rosa Amelia Plumelle from Colombia. The relationship between social achievement and class was highlighted by sociologists including Mary Pattillo from the USA and Stuart Hall from the UK, of Jamaican heritage.

Opinion shapers from a variety of backgrounds including artists and politicians[130] were the first to regard African hair as the major element in Black beauty. In Europe Black beauty blogs are the most developed and more numerous than other types of Black online

---

130. Dr Pole in her 2005 series of research articles.

presence. Mainly set in free platforms by women aged between 23 and 40, they require little training to be used. These platforms offer basic photo editing facilities and are smartphone-friendly. These details enable a 24 hour access to the photo sharing experience as well as a shortcut to the use of sophisticated equipment for quick updates. Beauty blogs are also one of the most popular types in the wider blogosphere. In our data collection, after having contacted about 50 of the most influential blogs across Europe, while a majority were claiming to cater for readers interested in beauty, only one blog was created by trained beauty professionals. After having recently read an article in a fashion news magazine[131] regarding a famous fashion blogger turned photographer who refused to join a well-known fashion publication to share her knowledge about social and online media because she wanted to keep her blog alive. This article may contribute to give a glimpse about how bloggers were initially considered experts in digital marketing. This storyline also suggests that the need for fashion magazines to update their practices by using classical business strategies including the market development strategy[132]. A business model which allows us to gain useful detailed market and competition intelligence as well as the incorporation of these data into the development of a new market segment. In other words fashion magazines, to supply their online demands (largely fulfilled by fashion bloggers at the time) decided to start describing as "digital expert" any citizen journalists or online influencers to join their team with a compulsory condition: they must stop their online website.

In general beauty bloggers are among the privileged elite of online opinion sharers: they are given free beauty products every day, they get to attend commercial launches, they get sponsorship opportunities for their own events and they receive payment to write about brands, events or people. This last aspect is often unspoken. Some bloggers admitted to have refused taking part in the survey as they did not

131. http://fashionista.com/2013/11/garance-dore-turned-down-position-at-important-french-magazine-to-keep-her-blog
132. Ansoff Matrix (1957).

wish their readers to know they were only writing or photographing brands, people or events which paid them generously just for a short write up or to use their faces for advertisements or to distribute free samples at beauty events. One of a recent series of scandals surrounding the blogging community was when a famous British Youtube blogger, Zoella, admitted to have used a ghostwriter for her sensational book released in early 2014.[133] The regulatory body in the UK has ordered online businesses, also known as blogs, to report if they have been paid to talk about a specific product. Failure to do so would be considered as a breach of the advertising code and would lead to legal action. Bloggers and vloggers claim that revealing that some of their posts were advertisements would reduce their viewership and damage their image.[134] This chapter will give some directions about how consumers may be misled while beauty professionals are worried about the consequences of unsafe and unethical beauty-based online activities.

The 19th and especially the 20th century have seen the start of the media explosion and of the mass production of cosmetics. Most of the "innovative" multinational companies in these fields originated in the United States and it is interesting to study the development of cosmetology for a mass market. The USA entered this field early due to a lack of access to water during the conquest of the West. Creating shortcuts when cleansing the body was essential to save water. Cosmetics had to be made efficient and easy to dissolve with little water. Demand for special products such as hair dye, toothpaste or toilet soap had to be made available to a growing market of consumers with or without an easy access to water. The cosmetics industry was set up at a time when the primary market was only in Western societies. Colgate-Palmolive was founded in 1806, Procter and Gamble in 1837, Avon in 1886, L'Oréal in 1909, Revlon in 1932. The first mass produced of skin care ranges were always advertised

---

133. http://www.theguardian.com/books/2014/dec/11/zoella-ghostwriter-sioban-curham-controversy-childrens-author
134. http://www.telegraph.co.uk/news/uknews/law-and-order/11255077/Hidden-advertising-by-vloggers-under-the-spotlight.html

and made for people living in these cultures. Developing ranges for colonized people who were at the time considered as non-consumers was useless. African cosmetics consisted of local organic products based often on religious traditions.[135] Until the introduction of modern hygienic methods, Africans used to identify women and men through the use of various forms of body art. The various stages of being a woman: puberty, marriage, childbearing, breastfeeding, menopause and widowhood, had specific skin patterns. New beauty criteria began to be accepted by the élite during the colonial period and the use of "African equipment" related to ancient practices was disparaged. Africans began to see Western cosmetics as "European" and therefore "civilized". Cosmetics multinationals started to take an interest in these emerging markets following the success encountered with beauty products sold to African-Americans. African-American demands at the time were the product of their Westernized environment and their social need to identify with European-Americans. African-Americans were witnessing the early stages of a growing and future global industry, the health, wellbeing and beauty industry. Nowadays, dark skinned women living in sub-Saharan countries tend to have African-American beauty practices ingrained into their routine as a consequence of both lack of interest in ancient African beauty practices and their ambition to appear as Westernized as possible, since Western ideas are promoted by local media as "modern."

In the UK, there are over 6 million non-European ethnic-minority people with an increase of 32% between 2001 and 2007[136]. Black people of Caribbean and African backgrounds represent less than two million individuals. As Leyla Ahuile underlined in her report for Mintel,[137] the difference between Black skin care and Black hair care should be fundamental to anyone trying to sell any beauty products to this market. Less impressed than other ethnic groups by the latest dermatological advances regarding skin rejuvenation or technology, they care for beauty products which do not irritate and seem as close

---

135. Beautifying the body in ancient Africa and today (2013).
136. Mintel, Ethnic Fashion Shopping Habits, July 2009 by Neil Mason.
137. Black and Personal Care Us, March 2011.

as possible to nature despite the numerous skin challenges they may encounter in a lifetime including acne, poor scarring of the skin, and lack of vitamin D. Black people in the UK favour high-quality brands as 33% of them shop in department stores.[138] The sudden multiplication of natural hair and skin care products now available to the UK Black online market can be explained by the need that was clearly identified by both business minded people and consumers, leading to the development of casual *beautypreneurs*,[139] *who are* often difficult to monitor and evaluate in official statistics. These days there is not one Black event in London which does not offer at least one of the so called "organic beauty brands" recommended by beauty bloggers or sometimes by magazines. This market of beauty products claiming to have been made using natural ingredients has given birth to thousands of imitations by various beauty business retailers. Lacking long term goals and market research, these retailers mislead the consumer in the image they may draw about Natural Ethnical and Organic (NEO) beauty products. As a result, these tend to simplify beauty businesses to the point that each consumer tries to set up and sell his or her beauty products and services overnight, creating missed business opportunities rather than establishing a business niche. The Black beauty blogosphere is no exception. Black and ethnic groups tend to have more access to the Internet than any other European minority living in the UK. This may be due to a tendency to use online communication as a way to exchange a few words with relatives living in different locations and to keep in touch with news from their home countries. In addition to this they are the people who are using the Internet as a business opportunity to market their services, products and brands. Black British people do buy online and this trend is growing stronger every year as the Internet is easily accessible, provides good value for money and has an international outreach.

Blacks, alongside other ethnic groups including East Europeans and Asians are perceived by high street fashion retailers to form a

---

138. Where to shop for clothing by ethnic origin, March 2009.
139. beauty+entrepreneurs=beautypreneurs.

majority of low income shoppers that is hard to target.[140] These brands have long ago stopped focusing on buying habits of ethnic minorities and prefer targeting the lifestyles of the majority of their Western customers and their income as primary sources of information to identify their market. With the growing Internet-based beauty business, these multinationals have also considered using online platforms to advertise and sell their products using some of the "brand new" online black businesses offering products, advice and services. Meanwhile, on the African continent, marketing of beauty is led by selling premium products such as perfumes and "miracle" hair products from top selling companies such as Procter and Gamble, L'Oréal and Unilever which monopolise the beauty market. The strongest emerging market for beauty in the African continent is South Africa which has consistently maintained growth with a network of distribution led by supermarkets. With its unique form of multiculturalism, South Africa may be the land of the next generation of beauty moguls and the scene of a globalized approach to African beauty practices.

In the Americas, Brazil is the self-proclaimed innovator for countries with Black culture. As part of the BRICS[141], Brazil has shown signs of regularity and knowledge regarding the cult of beautification. As the only country in the Americas with an estimated half of its population being of European origin and the other half of African ancestry, Brazil is home to two multinational companies producing beauty products. Ethically aware, the Brazilian consumer is a key player in Black consumer market research.

For the purpose of our blogs analysis, it was necessary to illustrate some global trends in the Black beauty market. This information allowed me to place the Black European beauty online market into both context and perspective. According to Tonya Roberts, multicultural analyst for Mintel, "Image is everything to Black consumers and they are keenly aware that hair plays a key role in how people

---

140. http://www.theguardian.com/media-network/media-network-blog/2013/jan/16/british-advertisers-ignore-ethnic-minorities
141. "The emerging markets" – Brazil, Russia, India, China and South Africa.

view them." I will try to answer a few of the following questions often raised when considering European-based black beauty online businesses as a whole:

- Is good design of beauty black blogs necessary to maintain hit levels?

- Are historical images and values important to Black consumers and should we identify them?

- Which online strategies are used by bloggers to reach their targets?

- What is the relationship of blogs to their Black European readership?

2. Marketing to a Black female readership

As explained in the first section, Black Europeans are greatly influenced in terms of imagery by the US-based Black market. American Black beauty blogs are particularly perceived as trend creators who influence trend setters on the "old continent". Beauty for the Black European is a lifestyle choice as well as a lucrative business venture. Online beauty businesses targeting a Black niche market are expanding in an attempt to answer a growing demand which includes the kind of professional advice that only experienced beauty enthusiasts and beauty professionals can give. Thus Black beauty blogs have found an ideal location: neither retailers nor beauty therapists, hairdressers or makeup artists, they are citizens with a self-proclaimed passion for beauty. They are "beauty addicts."

Beauty blogs in the blogosphere are especially interesting to investigate as they are a meeting point of all the marketing strategies recently developed for online trade as well as a perfect example of fashion dissemination overcoming language, distances and cultures. To illustrate my hypothesis, I will assess the type of relationship the Black European beauty blogosphere may have with its readership. The power of beauty blogs is made up of several signs and codes.

They are related to visuals, narrative, and the sequence of these images and the words accompanying them. I will analyse their business strategies as to how and why they choose the Internet as a communication tool. "Since language is the most fundamental and pervasive medium for human communication, semiotics takes the way that language works as the model for all other media of communication, all other sign systems [...]." Here Bignell refers to the different types of language used to interact with human beings. He introduces the application of concepts such as "language-based media" and "image-based media." In fact, he goes as far as the origin of the science behind signs: the semiotics theorized by both the Swiss scholar Ferdinand de Saussure (1857-1913) and the American Charles Peirce (1839-1914). They largely investigated signs within societies. Media, being one of the most influential ways to disseminate information, uses sign systems to get the message across. Social groups, gender, age, location and culture enable those in control of media dissemination to define which type of narrative will be best to communicate ideas, concepts and opinions. Only the pre-conception and codes used to identify objects, emotions or anything else within a language have the power to shape images in people's mind. If we take the example of the word "*Afropolitanism*" (chapter 1), three writers defined it differently according to their personal experiences: for some *Afropolitanism* is about location, for others about lifestyle and for a third category it is more about a mind-set. All are using English as a language to express their views on the subject because they feel confident enough to have profoundly understood each concept they present. The black European-based beauty blogosphere is based on several factors including:

• Intense use of photography also called photojournalism or photo essays

• Publication in reverse time

• Continuity between each post and each subject

• Desire to exchange ideas and converse with their readers

All of these factors, can be referred to as codes; the codification of systematically supplemented text –or lines with photography– while telling stories on a regular basis is called photojournalism. Initially used by photographers working with printed media, this approach was launched by photographer Cartier-Bresson (1908-2004). The idea refers to complementing text with imagery to create greater appeal in the mind of a targeted readership. The use of blogs is a continuation of these practices. As Bignell[142] wrote: "[...] photographic media seem to be more realistic than linguistic media [...]." In the context of beauty blogs, these online platforms showing extensive personal images support the viewers in the dissemination of personal experiences. The readers tend to identify more with simple language and signs. This attitude therefore breaks down to some extent the professionalism shown by accredited and trained beauty journalists and professionals. Bloggers seem to appear in competition with mainstream media since they are not part of that sphere; they create proximity with their readers and followers based on their emotional needs[143]. A good example was the January 2012 confrontation between a famous Black French blog and a well-established international French magazine[144] which published an article about how Black women in France decided to become stylish after the arrival of Michelle Obama at the White House. The hundreds of blog viewers felt insulted: according to the magazine, Black French women only became interested in fashion because the American First Lady served as an inspiration to them, thus suggesting that Black French women had not changed since the early 20th century when they were most likely to emulate American standards of beauty. An open letter sent by the blog to the magazine led to a filmed explanation from their editor to the bloggers which was broadcast on their YouTube channel and the removal of the offensive article.

Often expressing views using technical jargon and speaking with authority, beauty executives and journalists are nowadays challenged by

---

142. See page 70.
143. Deborah Gabriel (2014) Blogging while Black and British: An exploratory study on the use of Blogs as social cultural and counterhegemonic practice.
144. http://www.respectmag.com/2012/01/25/afrosomething-lettre-ouverte-au-magazine-elle-5942

amateurs branded as beauty or media professionals. "Amateurism sells. The more unofficial the message, the more likely the consumer will take ownership of it."[145] How does this translate in terms of business? As presented in the next diagram, a trend, such as Natural Afro hair, is branded according to beauty bloggers as coming from the USA.

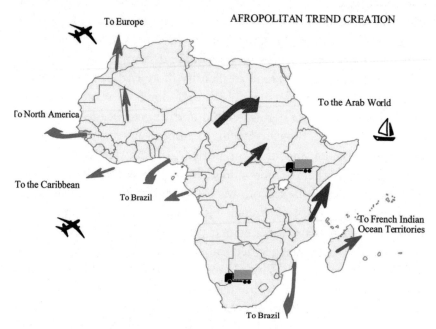

Adding cultural value to an Afropolitan trend (C. Kedi, 2014)

The original trend creators of the movement towards natural Afro hair were mainly Africans who travelled to the United States as early as the end of World War II. The trend setters were primarily the US artists and intellectuals who had travelled to Europe and to Africa to share their experiences as Black people in America and learn about the motherland.[146] They brought back to the USA[147] the a Afro comb

145. The Cult of the Amateur: How blogs, MySpace, YouTube, and the rest of today's user-generated media are destroying our economy, our culture, and our values (2008) by Andrew Keen.
146. African Hairstyles: Styles of Yesterday and Today (1984) by Esi Sagay.
147. Origin of the Afro comb exhibition (2012) by Sally-Ann Ashton.

and natural hairstyles. Many of these first trend setters were also cultural activists and performers. Women such as Miriam Makeba (1932-2008) and Nina Simone (1933-2003) were among the earliest to disseminate an idea of natural, holistic lifestyles. Trend creators can only build on solid cultural history and traditions. Trend setters are the first group of people to see a novelty in what is old or even very ancient. Historians and archaeologists have illustrated the beginning of afro hair combing and care in the ancient African traditions yet there is still an aversion to coarse afro-hair textures expressed in the Black European blogosphere. How does this misinterpretation of the African cultures translate into what seems to be a productive online business model? It would be beneficial to assess the effectiveness of the tools used in this business strategy. The strengths, weaknesses, opportunities and threats (SWOT) are illustrated in the diagram below.

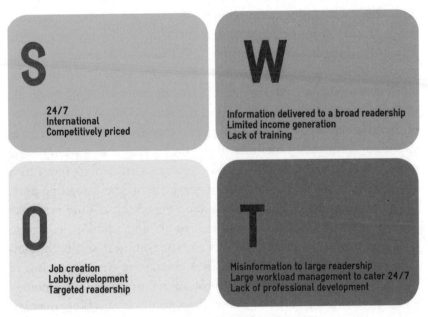

S

24/7
International
Competitively priced

W

Information delivered to a broad readership
Limited income generation
Lack of training

O

Job creation
Lobby development
Targeted readership

T

Misinformation to large readership
Large workload management to cater 24/7
Lack of professional development

SWOT analysis for Black beauty bloggers (C. Kedi, 2015)

Beauty blogs are one of the most successful influencers in Europe. Out of the twenty-five bloggers we interviewed, four out of five described their activities as "blogging about beauty". The most relevant cases were in European countries with a large population of people of African origin: France, UK, Spain, Germany and Portugal. The SWOT analysis shown above will enable a more accurate evaluation of the online strategies used by some of these influencers. Considering their most common strengths; the first would be their availability on an online system that can be viewed at a low cost by many throughout the day and night, as internet access in Europe is widespread. The content can be accessible internationally from a variety of devices including mobile phones, computers, tablets and some interactive TVs. Among the tools used are smartphones, digital cameras and creative software enabling the use of illustrations, video and photography for a more accurate display of information, and opinion.

The weaknesses include a lack of training in modern technology; difficulties of accessing online content due to poor infrastructure; and a lack of interest in the blog content resulting in a limited readership primarily in the northern hemisphere. Viewers often merely scan the content instead of reading it which leads sometimes to a misunderstanding of an unsourced content. People can end up misinformed due to their lack of patience and critical thinking. The last consequence of these weaknesses is when a blogger moves from opinion sharer as an online community member to the endorsement of a professional role despite a lack of training. Readers are attracted to blogs as a source of data which they expect to get in the shortest possible time. Bloggers are under pressure to maintain viewership. Some even risk presenting themselves as specialists, experts and opinion leaders to keep up the number of blog viewers and the comment section of their blogs active. Legal issues can occur as there have been rare cases of bloggers being accused of using a professional name and terminology without permission. One of the weakest points of this blogging activity is auto-control: when does a blogger decide to undertake the role of a professional to advise his or her viewers on questions they raise? Bloggers see opportunities of business development in these roles as consultants and opinion leaders. Beauty bloggers raise interest among manufacturers of beauty products targeting a niche market such as Black women in Europe. In fact, to access this specific market some of these brands have partnered with successful Black bloggers to raise their global profiles by using their products to influence their viewers. Presented as celebrities, these bloggers obtain a larger influence over their followers. This will only work as long as the readership keeps seeking miraculous beauty products rather than trying to understand that both a beauty regime and the hands of beauty professionals may lead to more positive results. Beauty bloggers know how to maximize their influence and their viewer's online experience.

The opportunities are as online community and marketing developers. Bloggers know how to build databases of selected sections of markets according to the type of subjects they cover online. They also know how to influence those readers while producing information quickly, and seemingly possessing an independent opinion.[148] Bloggers seem to represent a new breed of online business developers ready to use a combination of social marketing skills, social media tools, SEO search, branding and fashion imaging to complement their vision. Marketing to a Black female readership is about understanding the demand, living in a fashion capital, and creating a sensational effect of individualism. The threats are linked to the weaknesses: the risk of misinformation when the readership is too large, a workload that is not sustainable 24/7 and a lack of professionalism. Amateurism in online content generation can thus be used a marketing strategy, gaining the the trust of Black female readers by responding to their need for an online "next door girl" perhaps perceived as an online friend turned "celebrity".

3. Celebrity, influence and social media

We have seen that Black beauty bloggers are the most successful among their peers in the USA and Europe. They are also the most recognized as the face of the natural hair movement ("nappy").

---

148. Generation Bloggeuses by Miss Phit (2012) p. 110.

These opinion sharers have moved from a position of citizen journalist, amateur writer or photographer to become online personalities. We can now define what an influencer is. This will allow us to illustrate why bloggers cannot qualify as celebrities and how social media can reduce them to the same level.

According to Chong Ju Choi and Ron Berger in their 2009 article,[149] the decrease in social and community-driven activities in favour of social online actions results from a celebrity culture. They have developed an addiction to fame through their online communities. Research on contemporary American youth assessed the influence of online social communities in life, politics and entertainment. Several books and articles have been written which acknowledge the risks of using the Internet as the main source of information for an entire generation.[150] Market research companies including Mintel in their report of September 2010, "The Empowered Consumer," and again in "Household internet access levels by ethnic group" (2008) are also relevant. In all cases, whether US or UK based, the trends were all about protecting the consumer from citizen journalism, Internet cyber-crimes and poorly managed e-commerce platforms.

The use of social media by some celebrities and bloggers to conceptualise fame as a day to day practice was also debated by some of these writers including the risks occurred by such practices in the world of business. In their article, Choi and Berger add to their list the "bandwagon effect" where a craze for a particular product or products is created. They describe this as one of the most elaborate threats to marketing, e-marketing and advertising ethics related to the use

---

149. Ethics of global Internet, community and fame addiction in Journal of business ethics.

150. These authors included Andrew Keen (2007), Theresa Senft (2008) David Giles and Donna Rockwell who wrote "Being a Celebrity: a Phenomenology of Fame (2009) Journal of Phenomenological Psychology (2009) p. 178-210. Also Alice Marwick and Dana Boyle (2011); also "To see and to be seen. Celebrity practice on Twitter" (2011): The International Journal of Research into New Media Technologies 17(2) 139-158. "To see and to be seen. Celebrity practice on Twitter" (2011): The International Journal of Research into New Media Technologies 17(2) 139-158. Also Catherine Knight Steele (2012)

of the Internet. It is a dominant practice among top Black bloggers since it supports the practice of content sharing, trend creation and product review. The natural hair "movement" is the best example of the bandwagon effect. Due to content sharing about Afro hair in the early 2000s in the USA, the first Black bloggers who imitated their American peers, appeared in the mid-2000's.

As we described earlier the dissemination of trends is closely related to the hierarchy of influence among Black communities worldwide. What city-based Americans find trendy is automatically adopted in Black Europe. As trend diffusers these beauty bloggers became attracted to lifestyle and fashion and the bandwagon effect highlighted some early online personalities. Chosen because of the lack of interest in social media by both beauty professionals and the beauty media in the early 2000s, the beauty bloggers decided to "fill" the gap by spreading news coming from the USA. In our survey the few bloggers who admitted making a living from their online platform were mainly beauty bloggers. This new concept may inform the views of Andrew Keen (2007) about the culture of "Ego-casting" which could be translated as an online celebrity status attributed to top bloggers.

Ego-casting grew out of this trend. Here are life examples of bloggers who refused to take part in this evaluation. For these reasons, their names cannot be revealed but the locations are real. Assessing their market development or market penetration strategies is based on Ansoff matrix (1957). Due to the new phenomenon created by blogger "A" in Paris, companies started to give away samples to be tested. Blogger "B" started an online platform. Quickly photographs and videos flourished to share how to use all of these products, good or bad. By the time bloggers "C", "D" launched, the bloggers "A" and "B" have already gained a certain following which they were not willing to share. After a couple of years, some of these joined newly-formed online magazines, others became vloggers while a third and limited group set up online boutiques. Due to their lack of training in media, many beauty bloggers were using limited resources to spread their "findings" on the net. Practice with the media gave more confidence to some of these beauty bloggers to the point that they started displaying a certain egoism. Ego-casting is a consequence of this phenomenon:

aware of their growing influence on online communities, beauty bloggers began to ego-cast. According to Marwick and Boyd (2011)[151], the celebrity status is managed through the relationship between the fans and the celebrity; through the interactions among celebrities; and through the management of intimacy.

New technologies have reshaped the perception and definition of what celebrity is. The "blogebrity"[152] has grabbed online attention in the last few years just by telling the readers about his or her personal thoughts. Blogs, online communities, gossip sharing and the existence of celebrities – all have to take into account the user generated content. The last century's media (TV, radio, newspapers, magazines and PR companies) which allowed the admission of celebrities onto the wall of fame now have to share their power with blogs. Celebrity management in 2016 is about communication with fans, intimacy displayed and VIP contacts. Fame is a business strategy to either produce or maintain a fan base. The attributes of celebrity include having a huge following of fans, being recognised by peers (other celebrities) and promoting oneself (ego-casting). The celebrity is a cultural phenomenon, a media product. According to Theresa Senft (2008)[153] bloggers, social media users and more generally online content generators have generated a "celebrification process" by acting like celebrities. The democratization of online media has enabled the power of self-gratification, ego-appraisal and celebrity-like construction. Senft showed that the nature of social media and the practice of celebrity creation used by online content generators, despite the on- and offline self-branding activities and the number of followers, does not qualify them to be celebrities. She referred to them as "micro-celebrities". She described attributes of micro-celebrities as:

- Using celebrity as a practice
- Strategic self-presentation

151. Alice Marwick and Danah Boyd. (2011). "The Drama! Teen Conflict in Networked Publics."
152. A person who gained media attention because of his/her blogging. The quick expert guide to writing a blog (2012) Plaja, Luisa, p. 8.
153. Camgirls: Celebrity & Community in the Age of Social Networks (2008).

- Considering friends and followers as a fan base
- Targeting popularity as a goal

Top social media actors remain the conventional celebrities including political leaders, those in the entertainment industry and others. What makes bloggers influencers rather than celebrities is the absence of the back-up which supports the reality of being a celebrity. The back-up is ultimately what makes a celebrity a cultural phenomenon, attending concerts and events. Bloggers share similarities with celebrities in that they have fans and a certain status in the media but their fans tend to be from a niche group and are found by word of mouth rather than through traditional media. They may have some interviews in the press but rarely with national channels or radio stations.

Privacy sharing among celebrities is typically about the moment they are "off" stage, "off" screen and still exist as a brand for any type of media. They may pre-date the Internet and they are likely to be recognisable by people unconnected to the Internet. Bloggers are not always associated with a cultural phenomenon despite the fact that they attend VIP events and are closely related to the Internet and the explosion of social media. For all these reason we call them "blogebrities" or micro-celebrities. Giles and Rockwell (2009) stated that a differentiation should be made between a famous person and a celebrity. These terms do not mean the same as people in both categories are aware of their status and behave accordingly. Fame is more about a mass society phenomenon, an urban glorification of certain historical figures. Celebrity is more about a person built up by the mass media in a contemporary context. That is the reason why "celebrity" is even applicable to micro-celebrities such as bloggers. The state of fame can be divided into four phases: love/hate; addiction; acceptance; and adaptation. The love/hate phase is a constant process going through the cycle creating the "fame" factor. Famous people enjoy the recognition but many hate the loss of privacy. They have to put up with constant judgment and scrutiny from others.

The addiction phase is about the behaviour of the person's admirers who have demanding expectations. The acceptance phase is related to the daily changes which have to occur to move from a "regular" citizen to a famous person. It is about adapting to wealth, living with the fame factor including the personal struggles that are likely to affect family and acquaintances that have become targets for gossip. There is often mistrust of those around. Finally the adaptation phase is the adoption of a lifestyle by famous people which can sometimes mean becoming reclusive and sometimes lonely in order to maintain some peace.

While some top bloggers deliberately put themselves into this category, they do not really fit. As influencers they support people in the choices that suit their best interests. They are bonded to their followers because of the "girl next door" companionship they provide. Nevertheless some of them are perceived as famous brands or personalities. They use endorsements to sell products, services and dreams supported by S-commerce[154] and F-commerce.[155] Celebrities get paid to endorse a brand while bloggers tend to get endorsements without necessarily acknowledging the sponsoring of their product. The taboo around business ethics and money relationships is a blogger-related issue, not a celebrity one. An online influencer faces the problem of how to behave when it comes to money making and how to manage their relationships with their followers. Researchers Berger and Choi argue that social and community interrelations have seen the growth of a cult of fame and celebrity. They ask how we can measure the potential effects on business ethics of the growing influence of the celebrities on the Internet. Although they focus on celebrities' endorsements, their analysis can be applied to top bloggers. People who tend to follow bloggers are making purchases without always realising why – "Herding occurs when a consumer's choice depends on the decisions of others"[156] "One key way in which information is diffused globally today is through word-of-mouth communication, through social and community networks on the worldwide web."[157]

---

154. Subscription commerce.
155. Facebook commerce.
156. Ethics of Global Internet, Community and Fame Addiction (2008).
157. Hodgson, 2003; Negus, 2002; Schelling, 1978; Seaman, 2003; Smith, 2001.

Choi and Berger explain that: "In the 21st century, such choices are increasingly made by celebrity endorsement effects and the association with people who are 'internet famous.'"[158] Young people are the main victims of this Internet business and marketing tool which offers information fast and at low cost. According to the 2009 report of the American Federal Trade Commission,[159] bloggers who endorse products without admitting it to their readers are violating the law.[160] This is also the case in France where financial penalties can be incurred.[161] This policy can also inform the business aspects of these online tactics: surveys can give from customers or from the targeted market. Consequently, when assessing the e-commerce strategies among top leading black bloggers in Europe, surveys may support the analysis.

To conclude, celebrity, influencer and social media are all related. They use similar steps to operate at different levels and serve different purposes. Black bloggers are using some of the social media strategies and tactics used by famous people and celebrities to achieve similar status. This comforts their relationships with readers, advertisers and peers. Celebrities are using social media to maintain their social status and keep their fan base updated. Black bloggers are qualified as micro-celebrities, influencers and social media content generators. The development of technology to facilitate online interaction has led to the burgeoning of social media including User Generated Content (known as UGC). UGC is "a wide variety of media content that is produced by [...] audiences as opposed to content made by the BBC. [...] UGC has expanded due to developing technologies that are now readily available, including digital video and images, mobile text messages, blogging, message boards, emails and audio submissions."[162]

---

158. Ethics of Celebrities and Their Increasing Influence in 21st Century Society (2009).

159. http://www.ftc.gov/sites/default/files/attachments/press-releases/ftc-staff-revises-online-advertising-disclosure- guidelines/130312dotcomdisclosures.pdf

160. http://www.socialmediaexplorer.com/social-media-marketing/disclosures-for-bloggers-and-brands/ (Avril 2013)

161. Article L. 213-1 du code de la consommation.

162. Myers (2009).

To better understand the different mechanisms and steps to undertake while creating a buzz around services or products using the blogosphere as a main marketing strategy, we will analyse examples of beauty brands and their relationships with some of the most successful blogs on the net. Acting as trend creators, they present the products as being new to the market. Having had the privilege of attending the launch of new ranges of manufactured goods, the beauty blogs move to the point of setting up the trend of a new generation of hair treatments. Here is an overview of the implications of the large network of influence that these female opinion leaders generate. Ansoff Matrix[163] provides information regarding the strategy operated by these bloggers to sell their products and services to a specific market using online tools.

Social commerce example of strategy for the blogosphere (C. Kedi, 2015)

---

163. Ansoff matrix (1957).

Social commerce (sometimes referred to as subscription commerce) is one of the most discussed business models as it is born out of e-commerce. It is the art of using social media to make business deals using strategies such as the ones shown above. Among these approaches, this one is the common way to identify and evaluate the impact of the online marketing and sales for a specific product or service: the six Cs.[164] The six Cs are namely:[165] customer, consistency, communication, creativity, culture and change. The customer is known by the blogger as a "real" person as opposed to the traditional market research which defines him as a business subject using demographics and psychographics. The consistency means using the same message over and over on the blogger's platform. This technique is also known in the business world as integrated marketing communication. Its creativity is about informing (by the use of blog posts about latest trends) and persuading by creating myths. A good example is when Black beauty bloggers created the "myth" of accrediting the origins of relaxing African hair to Black America. Finally, creativity can also be used to remind people about the blogger's own reality by constantly reminding the readers about using logos or specific "trademarks" such as a way of dressing or speaking. The blogger must communicate effectively using semiotics and cross-cultural references for a specific readership. This communication translates the marketing into a valuable storyline rather than a direct call to buy. Lastly, the change considers the capacity to adapt to the political, economic, social, technological, environmental and legal (also known as PESTEL) framework and adapt the marketing strategy accordingly. This theory supports the understanding of the social media scene applied by Black bloggers. Once they have learnt how to use social media, the bloggers can follow the requests and suggestions raised by their readers and adapt their marketing to sustain a consumer-centric marketing.

The development of new generations of bloggers called *vloggers*[166] is a further step in the strategy of improving communication with a consumer market. Started by bloggers, this trend has now hit beauty

---

164. Also known as consumer-centric marketing.
165. Source: www.entireweb.com by Michael Brito.
166. Video bloggers.

retailers who have witnessed the combination of the lack of physical interaction and the two-dimensional experience that social media can offer: with the Internet, there is no way to physically test or try out the products. Tutorials started by African-American bloggers with simple technology have raised millions of viewers for some vloggers. Sponsored in kind by manufacturers and through constant advertising so that the number of viewers has constantly grown, these opinion leaders have organised events to create a "three dimensional" experience (m-commerce),[167] meeting their followers in person. The bloggers eventually convert the few who are still reluctant to buy online into e-commerce addicts. These influencers end up offering styling services through tutorial videos at discounted prices for the subscribers on both the blog and the online channel (s-commerce).[168] The marketing strategy is constantly maintained and monitored through the use of f-commerce.[169] Well organised, some bloggers and vloggers may have followers reaching millions of people (on average it takes three years to attain tens or hundreds of thousands of hits daily). The largest blogs have been around since the early 2000s and, as pioneers, they are leaders in the industry, reaching micro-celebrity status in France for example. What is surprising is that despite operating in fashion cities like London and Milan they choose to portray on average 95% of their styling role models using African-American celebrities, neglecting their own original cultures or role models.

Different types of roles, jobs and other trades and professions are listed as part of the beauty industry. They are interrelated: a beauty editor needs to know the trends and write about the principal features of the moment since the survival of the magazine depends on the advertisements and the readership. A manufacturer of beauty products will need to work with suppliers, service providers and cosmetologists to create a brand to serve the public demand with the help of beauty press. Now beauty consumers are protected by a consumer legal framework and some lobby groups campaign against poor service, challenging beauty products and unprofessional practices by both

---

167. Mobile commerce.
168. Subscription commerce also sometimes referred as social commerce.
169. Facebook commerce.

beauty practitioners and sellers. The beauty consumer may have some influence through purchasing power and sometimes through lobbying.

BEAUTY INDUSTRY AND CONSUMERISM

Beauty industry and surroundings (C. Kedi, 2015)

In the above diagram the professional industry is characterized by skilled people with obligations and defined roles in their professional activities. Most beauty professionals have to join an industry or trade organization which manages and regulates the code of practice within the profession as explained in my recent book.[170] Similarly, beauty marketers are people who create an image of beauty according to different influences including culture, the fashion industry, media and consumer demands. They are not beauty practitioners but they still belong to the beauty industry since they play an important role in the dissemination of beauty trends to the general public. Beauty influencers and beauty consumers are similar. Beauty influencers, because of their proximity to beauty marketers tend to think they are part of the industry but they do not provide training, develop services or have sufficient knowledge to belong. Bloggers who assert themselves as experts seem to ignore the fact that expertise includes training, experience in the field and practice in the industry. Anyone can try out free samples of beauty products but should not promote them until the goods are agreed in terms of quality checks and marketing strategies. Beauty influencers are then invited to promote the latest findings. This is where confusion seems to occur. Some bloggers think that because they had exclusive access to a product before it reached the general public they belong to the beauty industry.

Some US based-bloggers, consumers setting up an online personal diary, give rise to myths. One is that there are African-American hair types. There is no evidence to claim an "African-American" type of hair but science recognises both "Indo-European" and "African" hair types.[171] Another concerns miracles of hair growth with products made from ingredients contested by professional bodies – hair grows from the inside out therefore food, heredity and lifestyle are the main

---

170. Beautifying the Body in Ancient Africa and Today by Christelle Kedi (Books of Africa, 2013).
171. Loussouarn G (August 2001). "African hair growth parameters". Br. J. Dermatol. 145 (2): 294-7

indicators for healthy growing hair.[172] Confusion between natural and organic products is also raised,[173] as is natural African hair type. Afro hair and hair colour are genetic traits.[174]

The average consumer following some of these blogs may end up with an even more confused view about hair care. Hair care is a favourite subject among Black blogs worldwide. People sometimes follow Internet consumers who have tried some well-marketed products without taking a specialist's advice. This is how an entire industry is missing out on the basic principles of creating a successful trade. Many have claimed that some hairdressers have damaged their hair but a few have recognized that some manufactured products that are called "natural" can use any marketing slogan to advertise their products. In reality, the American Federal Trade Commission[175] is not allowed to approve cosmetic ingredients under the FD &C Act[176] except for a few ingredients such as coal-tar hair dyes or colour cosmetics. The only valid option is personal research and investigation. Bloggers have a role in the beauty industry since they allow direct feedback and interaction with the general public but their expertise in beauty products trials is only possible after the trade industry and professionals have approved the products made available to the distribution channels. Many products do not actually reach the shelves because beauty professionals who test them are not satisfied. Keeping an eye on blogs set up by beauty professionals and the blogosphere is a secure approach to the online hair care experience. The reliability of the blogosphere relies on several factors. There is a great temptation

172. Khumalo NP, Gumedze F (September 2007). "African hair length in a school population: a clue to disease pathogenesis?". Journal of Cosmetic Dermatology 6(3): 144-51

173. Greenwood, Norman N.; Earnshaw, Alan (1997). Chemistry of the Elements (2nd ed.).

174. Davenport, G. C., and C. B. Davenport. 1909. Heredity of hair color in man. American Naturalist 43: 193-211.

175. Source: www.ftc.gov

176. Source: http://www.fda.gov/regulatoryinformation/legislation/federalfood-drugandcosmeticactfdcact/

among bloggers to try to survive financially by accepting product endorsements or services. Internet based business is one of the most innovative and challenging areas of trade. The customer service experience, the sales of goods or services, the distribution channels, the advertising, the finances and human resources are all redefined in this previously unknown industry which seems to attract more business ventures every day. In a recent interview with a famous blogger, a fashion publication business manager acknowledged some of the numerous needs and risks taken by her business in an attempt to run both an online and offline fashion platform. She has described the difficulties the fashion industry experienced in investing in online platforms.[177]

177. Source: http://www.garancedore.fr/en/2012/01/31/career-girl-caroline/

Chapter IV
Black fashion blogs

Business is to blogs what the Internet is to computers: a sibling. The commercial nature of many of these online platforms is constantly reinforced through the marketing of some of their contents. They may assure their readers that all comments and opinions are totally independent unlike blogs managed by professionals in their fields which are not required to specify their independence. The number of sponsored links, advertisements and corner images appearing on blogs give another signal to both readers and researchers that bloggers are in business with a purpose, a vision and a mission. Whether the final aim is to become famous, to be an expert in the field or to promote the services they offer, it is in all cases still about business. Business strategists including Porter and Ansoff[178] defined business strategies as means to obtain specific ends for a long term plan. In other words, planning of long term goals is crucial for business survival. We saw earlier that beauty bloggers were Afropolitans living in fashion cities that have a clear view about online beauty business. They are also well aware of how to position their brand, image and online presence to uplift their profiles to attract more advertisers and followers. In this chapter, we will analyse how black fashion blogs define strategies and goals to get effective results.

178. Porter, M.E. (1980) Competitive Strategy, Free Press, New York.

1. Fashion blogs: street styling and selfies

As for their European counterparts, African-American female blogs are at the heart of the digital experience for US-based Black women since they share views and information about a number of subjects. These discussions address issues affecting their peers and, if managed adequately, create a buzz which seems to give them more credibility within their niche markets. As mentioned by Andrew Keen: "the real value of citizen journalism was its ability to address niche markets otherwise ignored by mainstream media". As opinion leaders, they choose topics and manage debates and discussions on specific subjects, often ignoring the experts or specialists on the subject pretexting "[…] that their amateur status allows them to give […] a less-biased, less-filtered picture of the world than […] from traditional news […]". With 181 million blogs globally[179], Technorati[180] suggests that blogs related to lifestyle categories represent the largest group. Entertainment, business, technology and sport are the other most read blogs. Technorati gives a general view on the blogosphere based on its search engine which tracks daily and hourly activities on about 1.3 million blogs worldwide.

We saw earlier why Black beauty blogs are successful among Black Europeans. They were initially set up by the first generation of bloggers in an attempt to answer the growing demand on hair and skin care issues amongst Black women. I would like to demonstrate how Black fashion bloggers, in comparison to their beauty colleagues, may be slowed down by the nature of the Western fashion industry which is an industry who sets icons. There are different types of fashion blogs, some targeting the fashion industry as a whole while others are more specific about the retail and clothing aspect of fashion and personal style. This latter includes street styling, personal styling and celebrity styling. These three types of blogs within the styling category are the most recognizable as they have given birth to micro-celebrities. Online micro-celebrities known for their style and looks are mostly dominated by personal styling blogs. Personal styling blogs are the best known since they enable the posting of raw looks presented by the blogger

179. Source: Nielsen report (2011) available on www.blog.nielsen.com
180. Source: www.technorati.com

to the viewers. Raw looks are looks achieved without necessarily applying the styling rules often seen in glossy magazines, on TV or in live shows. Within the category of street styling blogs despite the obvious gender separation, I would classify them as: art directed street styling, street styling, and personality street styling. Art-directed street styling refers to blogs in which the person pictured has been directed in some way e.g. posing, the location of shooting or transformed photography. This type of blog is common among fashion professionals who have set up blogs to express their perspective.

FASHION BLOGGING

Overview of Black Fashion blogging (C. Kedi, 2015)

These people do not necessarily use the blog to become celebrities but to share skills, get feedback about concepts and maybe collaborate or work with some people interested in their aesthetics. Celebrity blogging is often the offspring of fashion industry blogs.[181] Fashion vlogging, which is fashion blogging using moving images, film or video, is a way of sharing information, disseminating fashion industry news in practice around the world or locally. Such platforms tend to be owned or managed by professionally trained journalists, marketing executives or public relations officers. These blogs can also be the work of a collective of fashion professionals from all areas of the industry. They may have decided to source correct and valuable data related to the fashion world. In all cases, the desire to communicate and be noticed for particular reasons is the main characteristic for these online ventures. In a recent article in the London Evening Standard magazine,[182] Laura Craik wrote that some personal style bloggers were being offered huge salaries. Mainly followed on social media sites including Instagram and Twitter, these "blogebrities" seem to share a common formula for success: being pretty and stylish, having storytelling skills and the ability to create an emotional bond with the readers. Some mainstream fashion bloggers are millionaires. The same cannot yet be said of Black fashion bloggers in Europe.

Mainstream fashion blogging as a career grew up as a business idea. It was for fun and it became serious when it attracted hundreds of thousands of followers. The trends in fashion blogging are about celebrating a fashion-centered lifestyle presented as a fantastic life. So it is not surprising that this perception of fashion as a lifestyle was born in the USA in the late sixties.[183] The first founder of this trend was Ralph Lauren (1939-) when he launched his first collection in 1967 aiming to target every household in some way or another. The second was Calvin Klein (1942-) when he presented his tight fitting collection of jeans in 1974, opening a new era for this classic

181. The quick expert guide to writing a blog (2012) Plaja, Luisa, p. 8-9.
182. "Pretty girls + nice clothes= big business" by Laura Craik in Deluxe Standard. co.uk/lifestyle on 20th February 2015, p. 37-40.
183. Icons of fashion, the 20th century edited by Greda Buxbaum (1999 and 2005).

American product. While challenging the European status quo on fashion as an art form, these two fashion designers have since then greatly influenced the big new American names in fashion design including Michael Kors (1959-) and Marc Jacobs (1960-).

In the meantime, personal fashion bloggers who are keen on shooting selfies are likely to emulate the original ideas behind "street style". This look was launched in the sixties by young Americans who were teenagers just after the end of WW2. Celebrities who spread this style included Marlon Brando (1924-2004) and James Dean (1931-1955). The style was deliberately designed to refer to popular culture and to appear counter to mainstream culture, customizing high street brands but often using second hand clothes. In this context fashion bloggers sometimes choose street style clothing with photos shot in beautiful locations and styled by top hair and makeup artists.[184]

To understand what makes a fashion blogger get to the top of her game we need to try to evaluate the efficiency of top Europe-based Black fashion bloggers in their diverse strategies to reach their primary readership. Ahead of the fashion game are quite a few Europeans including: the Italian Chiara Ferragni, the Anglo-French Camille Charrière, the Swedish Elin Kling and the Swiss Christina Bazan. These are the most sought-after fashion bloggers online according to Fashionista's latest classification.[185] These "blogebrities" remain close to their original idea of blogging without necessarily adding categories not related to themselves. In her article classifying the 20 most influential bloggers,[186] Laura Sherman managed to take into account the followers on social media sites as well as hits per day on their blogs. Gaby Fresh was the only globally influential mixed-raced blogger. As a plus-size blogger, she also represented a certain demand. Does this mean that African-American bloggers do

---

184. "Pretty girls + nice clothes= big business" in Deluxe by Evening Standard (20th February 2014) p. 37-40.
185. Fashionista on 5th February 2015: http://fashionista.com/#!/2015/02/most-influential-style-bloggers-2015
186. Fashionista on 5th February 2015: http://fashionista.com/#!/2015/02/most-influential-style-bloggers-2015.

not reach high viewing numbers? Does it mean African-American women do not inspire fashionistas in the USA? Does this show a lack of interest or knowledge about Black fashion bloggers globally? Will European-based minorities have difficulty being represented? A few Asians were on the list but the ones that appeared were all living in the USA. This classification raises several questions related to the question of equality and diversity in Western fashion. Diversity should reflect the proportion of people living in a country and it is still not reflected in mainstream blogs. Western fashion does now seem to include the growing consumer market in Asia. Only two women of African descent, Iman Bowie and Lena Horne, have been accepted as fashion icons in the "International Hall of Fame,"[187] and the only mixed race blogger acknowledged by the top site classifying fashion blogs may be there to the fact that Gaby blogs for plus sizes.

This leads back to the debate related to the perception of style and beauty, and the relative absence of Black women in the fashion world. The "best dressed lists" were created in 1940 by fashion enthusiast and supporter Eleanor Lambert (1903-2003) and the international Best Dressed List was about acknowledging the American fashion between the two wars. In 1943 and 1962 she created the New York Fashion Week, which still presents collections from US-based fashion designers and The Council of Fashion Designers of America, Inc. (CFDA) which regulates and organises the trade in the American fashion industry. Her attempts to increase the visibility of American fashion were partly motivated when the Paris Fashion Week was stopped when the city was under German occupation.

Parisian designers were still willing to showcase their work to their American clients as well as their European counterparts who managed to escape the occupied territories. As the most affluent Public Relations in the fashion scene in USA, Eleanor Lambert, aware of the limited number of people who could afford European designers, launched this "best dressed list" to iconize these stylish people, initially from the European upper classes. She then extended the list to include celebrities of the time who thereby got media

---

187. International best dress list and hall of fame were created in 1940.

attention. Still today the "best dressed list" grants a stylish status to the nominees and an iconic status to the winners who become fashion icons and remain inspirational sometimes even for future generations. The small number of Black women in this "best dressed list" reflects both the socio-economic dynamics of America at the time and the reality of Western fashion attitudes. Even today not many Black women are perceived as stylish. The blogosphere is no exception. This was not always the case if we consider books and pictures by Casimir Zagourski (1883-1944) or Pierre Verger (1902-1996). Both photographers celebrated styles from different parts of the African diaspora when photography was still a hobby for explorers of Africa. As a matter of fact, this lack of realistic representation may have an impact on how the Black readership responds to mainstream fashion bloggers.

2. Citizen journalism

The launch of several originally Black magazines across the USA was all about creating platforms where images of Black people could circulate. It was not only about positive images. As the newest medium, the Internet has followed in the footsteps of the press and early TV: minorities appear sporadically and not proportionally to their numbers. Even fashion weeks and catwalks in sub-Saharan Africa have ignored diversity and attract a certain type of clientele which aspires to be as Westernised as possible. Although some of the top Black lifestyle bloggers may argue that their subject should not put them into niche markets, leading beauty and fashion bloggers in Europe have had to learn the hard way. Street styling for a Black fashion blogger does not always mean massive advertising campaigns and the attention their White counterparts may experience. This can be seen in the way they interact with their readership. While some of them might still be trying to display mainstream fashion designers and brands on their websites, the majority have taken the responsibility of featuring Afropolitan brands, trends and fashion to balance the Black beauty blogosphere which is over-exposed to manufacturers.

Black fashion blogging generates comments, attention and guidance for readers and we can consider that the Internet is used by Black bloggers as a means of transmitting culture. According to Thompson,[188] the media have developed a culture based on the content of communication they spread. The media also produce, store and diffuse information which is perceived as significant to the people broadcasting it.

James Slevin[189] argues that the Internet differs from traditional media in the way it creates brand new channels of exchange between people. The whole of society is transformed by the non-stop communication that the Internet offers, beyond temporality and space. Reality today shares communication space with a virtual world. For Slevin, a new culture has emerged from this new communication tool which needs to be considered as a culture of "self-formation," as both a real entity and as a virtual character. Other forms of media cannot apprehend these authenticities since they can be edited, cut or deleted. On the Internet nothing is totally lost. The construction of a virtual self implies a different relation with one's past or present. The virtual self is viewed as a permanent project to be perfected. Mediated interactions and globalization may lead people and online communities to become what Giddens[190] calls "pilgrims". For him the pilgrim the modern-age man who has to learn about writing his biography according to life choices that he made early in life. The pilgrim seems to be in control of his life in its smaller moments. Nevertheless, according to Bauman[191] today pilgrims are challenged by a fast moving society which no longer guarantees certainty. Basic needs such as jobs and shelter have become uncertain everywhere in the world. Giddens has classified the original pilgrim into four different types of people that the Internet can easily identify. The process of identification in the real world is subjected to space and

---

188. Thompson (1995), The Media and Modernity.
189. The Internet and Society (2000) p. 7.
190. Giddens, Anthony "The constitution of society".
191. Bauman, Zygmunt "Life in fragments".

time.[192] The Internet does not obey these laws and people might get lost in their online searches. The readership of Black blogs seems to be part of that class of pilgrims who are lost on the net, seeking identity, location, history and culture. The notion of time is controversial for some Black people in general as a consequence of their history,[193] their original cultural web had to be reconstructed. The Internet provides a brand new cultural opportunity to express bonds of identity. If we apply Slevin's[194] logic to Black bloggers, they are responsible for their self re-construction on the Internet. The Internet, he writes, has become a tool for self-formation and cultural appropriation. The word "community" has evolved thanks to online communities. According to Cavanagh[195] a community may have the influence to identify with an ideal uncorrupted society." Bloggers are influencers and the "online community" they connect with may or may not group around particular interests, campaigns or political movements. Online communities in the USA have inherited a culture of politics as they were organised about elections and Black representation.

As suggested by Lisa Nakamura,[196] "the matter of race in cyberspace has gone from not being talked about at all to being talked about very little". She introduces the idea that the Internet should be part of an international education project: cyber cultures, because of their impact in entertainment and the media, should be taught at a younger age to avoid misuse and to sustain critical thinking and rigorous analysis. In the case of a Black female readership, some top Black bloggers have taken advantage of the lack of difference that beginners may see between professional information and subjective sharing of information (also called citizen journalism). A Black

---

192. Specific Measurable Achievable Realistic and Timed.
193. Dalphinis, Morgan (1997).
194. The Internet and Society (2000) p. 172.
195. Cavanagh, Allison (2007) "Sociology in the age of Internet" p. 102-119.
196. In "cultural difference, theory, and cyberculture studies" (2006) in Critical cyber-cultures studies p. 29-36

female audience[197] is likely to form a relationship with the content. Femininity and motherhood are linked and communication recreates the real world in an online platform. O'Riordan talks about "digital beauties" in reference to virtual female "[s]heroes" in digital video games. However, we can translate her views into the imagery of top Black female bloggers. The latter are virtual beauties who share their best tips to enhance their readers' beauty experience and encourage them to try the same beauty products and routines. Finally, top Black bloggers practicing citizen journalism gain followers by altering some aspect of their identity to the best of their ability, presenting a more attractive virtual version of themselves.[198] Joining social media without the need to tell the truth reassures and encourages some younger people: they can alter photographs or change their location.

Black bloggers play a definitive role in their communities on and offline. As a two way communication[199] with real human beings, the answers from Black fashion bloggers are spontaneous. This is unlike a majority of beauty blogs that are co-managed by manufacturers who often require their PR and marketing departments to turn a debate into a product endorsement. Once a subject has been debated whether or not there is a definite conclusion, the fashion blogger may decide to organise events and invite beauty specialists. Set as pop up boutiques or market stalls the recipe works effectively. It is a regular formula observed on most of the successful fashion platforms. They operate according to the popularity of a subject as well as the traffic it may generate to their online site. These strategies alongside a few other techniques allow the fashion blogosphere to maintain a constant flow of information and discussion. The more people discuss and share views about a particular product, service or subject, the better the online presence and the hit rates. This tactic challenges the mainstream media or specialist by spreading true or false information

---

197. Gender, Technology and visual cyber culture (2006) in Critical cyber-cultures studies p. 243-254
198. None of this is real: identity and participation in Friendster' by Danah Boyd (2007) in structures of participation in digital culture.
199. A type of interpersonal communication.

across the net at high speed. Black fashion bloggers have to meet their readers in a more conventional manner: a talk or debate, a temporary boutique or styling service offered during a beauty event or a catwalk show is rarely a model for a campaign. The Black fashion blogger has to be more than just a woman sharing her views online about X or Y as beauty bloggers do. She has to write more, discuss more and show some level of craft, expertise or talent. Often these Black fashion bloggers have a background in the creative sector but not the majority. The top bloggers are rarely the ones trained in fashion journalism but like their non-Black counterparts, they comment about trade events including fashion weeks and celebrity styling options. Andrew Keen describes this phenomenon as amateur journalism.[200] He adds: "Despite the size of their readership, even the A-list bloggers have no formal journalistic training. And, in fact, much of the real news their blogs contain has been lifted from (or aggregated from) the very news organizations they aim to replace". For that reason, it is harder for a Black blogger to cover fashion as a subject on its own. A combination of all these factors generates a list of challenges that only knowledge, confidence and time can overcome. Here are some examples to illustrate situations I have witnessed during the 18 months I investigated blogs across Europe.

3. Three senarios

Scenario 1: "Blogger UK" has a contract with a Europe-based African TV channel because of the experience she gained as a model. The principal challenge this blogger faces is that despite the fact that she has been part of the industry for so many years, she has no formal training in fashion journalism or even in a media related subject; she studied politics. UK Blogger cannot write journalistic articles, fashion reports or styling boards. She has limited contacts within the industry, mainly of hair and makeup artists plus few photographers. She is not aware of the trade events where she lives, or how to book

---

200. The cult of the amateur.

them or to get a press pass, and after four months she lost her job as a TV presenter. She consequently terminated her blogging career as she could no longer face the constant online questioning about her lack of spontaneity while on TV. This scenario is a real life situation which has happened on several occasions. It shows that opportunities are offered to Black fashion bloggers on a more regular basis than for their beauty colleagues, who act more as the face of multinational brands. Black fashion bloggers also attract more interest in the African-orientated media since the demands for that type of programmme is growing. Knowledge and transferable skills would have made the crucial difference.

Scenario 2: Blogger "France" lives in the UK. She studied a fashion-related subject at a prestigious school of fashion. Being bilingual, she would like to move onto the next step. She is under 30, full of energy and knows 10 Afro-Caribbean designers. She decides to set up a magazine, initially online, to feature brand-new talents from the London creative scene. Fashion styling has to feature only "high end" designers and brands since this blogger would like to reach the entire spectrum of readers, not just Black people. The launch was a success with hundreds of people attending, including companies interested in buying some advertising space. Blogger "France" does not realise that blogging and journalism are not similar despite using the same type of media. Writing and photography does not transform online readers who have been used to getting free unsourced information into paying subscribers. Blogger "France" does not understand that a publication, whether online or not, needs to have creative direction but also an editorial line. After the first issue, the online magazine stopped due to lack of funding, lack of time and poor management. Black fashion bloggers from art schools also attract the attention of the industry. There are plenty of opportunities for collaboration for young graduates; this does not necessarily mean that a fashion journalism career can be built with friends or colleagues who are also lacking experience in directing a full time project.

Scenario 3: Blogger "Netherlands" runs a successful blog. She has reached micro-celebrity notoriety. She is invited to countless A-list events and mingles with the top bloggers in Europe. One day she admitted that despite her inspiring journey into the world of blogging, she felt disadvantaged in comparison to her fellows. Some would earn €10 000 a month for short talks about products easy to promote in their writing and photos, while she, under 25 at the time, was advised by manufacturers and PR companies to blog for plus-size readers. Frustrated, she decided to undertake a different path and embrace a brand new career as a lifestyle blogger. She has trained in a business school and does not agree that her buzz comes from her spontaneity and fashion interest rather than her lifestyle options. Blogger "Netherlands" does not consider that switching from one subject to another without any transition looks indecisive to some readers. She has kept both her blogs alive but lacks the confidence, the writing skills and the sustained drive to write about lifestyle lifestyles and she did not succeed in her attempt to attract manufacturers and brands to advertise on her brand new platform. The last time I viewed her lifestyle blog, the latest post was over three months old. To move from fashion to lifestyle, a gradual transition is required. This blogger should decide whether she wants to pursue a career because she is interested in fashion, because she wants to be famous or for the financial rewards.

In these three examples, we decided to protect the people by not revealing their identity. They are fashion bloggers who are seeking options to persevere in that field which is a daily struggle. What will the next few years offer us in terms of Black fashion blogging in Europe? Hopefully talented young women who truly embrace the fashion industry!

Chapter V
Black blogs' online strategies

1. Male blogging and fashion promotion: the suit

The Black gay community in London has influenced the number of colourful men's suits as a global trend. As a consequence of unspoken factors including identity, sexuality, location and style, a person's appearance seems to be the final element showing what can an individual say about him- or herself. Fashion, gender and culture could explain how history and geography affect the changing styles within a niche market. Thus, the suit plays an emblematic role in the evolution of chic menswear. Therefore for the purpose of this hypothesis, the chosen attire is the suit, and it illustrates the story of the Black Fashionisto first in London and in other European cities including Brussels, Paris and Milan. It was presented as an installation so as to make it a participative experience. Entitled "Itinerary of a Black Fashionisto 1948-2014" it studies the reality of Black trendy men in London using photography and case studies and the role of the law. It also reflects the complex relationship Black men may have with the fashion industry. The use of sociology, fashion theory, filmed interviews and display of clothes inform the narratives related to Black Fashionisti in general.

Finally, this work focuses on the experience of one real life character. It analyses the journey of the man as a creative professional in the fashion industry. His personal development, his sense of style, mainly documented by his fashion illustrations of colourful suits in various books and magazines. His work has enabled me to reconstruct the history of the development of colourful suits among Black men in 2014. He symbolises the contemporary global trends in menswear from an Afropolitan perspective. This Black Fashionisto is an accomplished citizen of the world. Educated, well-travelled, well-connected and recognized for his work, this 2014 hero is a Generation X or Y man who may sometimes look back at what has achieved in his lifetime.

Many Lesbian Gay Bisexual Transexual (LGBT) activists have become Fashionisti and their voices are now heard worldwide. Visual research was the chief mode of assessment in this work. The findings taken from profiling leading Black fashion blogs in Europe during the spring of 2014 as well as the interviews with several Afropolitan boutique owners led to several questions being raised. Who were the male trend setters in Afropolitan Europe? What was the distinction between trend creators and trend setters for that specific niche market? What were the elements differentiating the Black British fashion scene and the Black European one for a male consumer? And finally how did these trends travel to Europe from Africa and vice versa?

To facilitate the primary research, photojournalism, displays and ethno-photography supported the growth of mood boards.[201] From this starting point, interviews revealed London-based looks in 2014 by adding words to images. The work was done using a collaborative approach in an attempt to answer the questions. Unable to find photography-based Black gay magazines in Europe, there was a need to provide publications for gay men. Some newspapers, community newsletters and commentaries concerning the evolution of the LGBT movement help us understand the double challenges that gay Black men had to overcome and have to face on a daily basis.

Writers such as Guillaume Dustan (2002) publicly defended the idea of defining this as using private space and preferences. He described in detail how "French private homosexuality" was different from the "American gay politicized" lifestyle. The first was attached to the idea of private space not known to the outside world while the second was about promoting LGBT rights in the public space by defining oneself primarily through sexual orientation. The debates around LGBT rights eventually resulted in the reinforcement of punitive laws in most African countries causing those minorities to suffer difficult lives. Patrick Awondo explained: "Paris, London, New York are just the continuation of a migration process which aims at finding safer

---

201. also known as inspirational boards and popular among fashion professionals.

places for gay people". Not yet labelled Black British, nor English or Caribbean, this man grew up in an era of reconstruction and restructuration in Europe. Its society, economy and lifestyle were to take a clear new direction with the development of imagery through television and modern photography techniques.

The Black gay people in South Africa "still feel a high level of intolerance within their communities" according to Van Wyk (2006) despite spotting that most participants to his study admitted that they "… like being seen at fashionable spots". The recent TV advertisement for an international Irish stout showing *sapeurs* as main characters was globally well-received by their European-based communities.

As mentioned by Awondo (2014) « Les *sapeurs* » are one of those African trends that succeeded in creating a global trajectory and influencing global fashion. " It also raises questions about the lifestyle of culturally-challenged African migrants in Europe who spend on average €2,000 a month to buy expensive suits. Their irresponsible lifestyle choices sacrifice the economic stability of their households for the appearance of success. Consequently, Foxton (2014) also identifies the adaptation of Western code of dress to and for an African market migrating to Europe: "Their use of colour is amazing, and some of the more extreme outfits are quite brilliant. But in essence they are not too different to many subcultures in the way that they adapt and subvert the dress codes of those in authority above them e.g. Teddy Boys and Mods". If based in Africa or the West Indies, the Sapeurs, Rudeboys and other Black Fashionistos act as trend creators. Soboye (2014) describes this Afropolitan fashion phenomenon as "Presenting a new upmarket version of Africa". Once they reached Europe, whether born there or through migration, they were qualified to be identified as Afropolitan trend setters.

Afropolitan identity is, according to Pelasi (2005), a mixture of an African heritage with and developed within a Western society. To Soboye (2014), Afropolitans are "people that have an Afrocentric vision. They travelled all over the world, they have an international lifestyle […] They are really African in their settings, aesthetics".

Still controversial, the choice of calling oneself Black British, while adopting an Afropolitan lifestyle (integrating elements of African culture in daily life) is presented here. The research process started with the mood boards to consider the sociological perspectives of the Black presence in London. While Black women are represented in the fashion industry, their male counterparts are still experiencing less coverage and sometimes more controversial representation. Foxton (2014) describes the phenomenon. "Generally black men have been portrayed as either exotic, dangerous or athletic, or a mixture of these. Not necessarily totally negative stereotypes in themselves but without the balance of more "normal" portrayals these images become disempowering." Furthermore, the change in social and economic circumstances for the first generations of Black migrants in UK in the 20th century had an impact on the transmission of dress codes to the contemporary Black male buyers. They inherited either a rejection of the status quo by dressing as Rastafarians or Rude Boys – or by trying to blend in as much as possible. Mostly attracted to England by a chronic lack of employment in the Caribbean, the majority of migrants were educated people who could afford to leave family, culture and home space to settle in England. As mentioned by Scott (2009): "Many lower-middle class people from the Caribbean, once they came to England, became working people, so there was a kind of class shift as you moved from the Caribbean [...]". As a result, Black styling became a personal and cultural journey. According to Boateng (2009), "Style is personal and as a reflection of who you are and your character".

Sapeurs and black Fashionisti in London according to personal stylist Agathine (2014) "[...] have been under-represented. As our society is evolving, there is recognition of the black contribution to music as well as fashion. For instance the street urban style is extremely popular all over the world for youth culture. And now the Rude Boy movement has returned." These seem to have been more visible in the 1970s and 1990s probably due to the influence of hip hop and street style. Nevertheless, with the explosion of urban culture worldwide ethnic minority consumerism in clothes encountered several challenges including lack of sizes fitting their body types, housing problems, living far from high street shops in the town centres. Finally high street chains do not seem to consider ethnic minorities as a profitable market. This trend is confirmed by Sylvain when he says, "Well, I have been dressing men for the past ten months and remember dressing a Black man only once. Maybe this demonstrates their macho "I can do it myself" attitude."

2. Business development strategies and tactics

Conquering a bigger space, moving to another country, translating blogs into one or several foreign languages all have a common purpose: getting into a new market. As part of a business strategy, these tactics are relevant for top bloggers who have reached maturity in their life cycle. By maturity I refer to the traditional product life cycle theory which was initially described as: "The period of time over which an item is developed, brought to market and eventually removed from the market"[202]. The product life cycle theory is an offspring of business strategies introduced in a different form by Ansoff (1918-2002)[203]. In the previous chapter, we evaluated the location, identities, habits, expectations and social media use of some of the top Black bloggers in Europe. In this chapter we will concentrate on the business side of blogging. As we suggested above it is important to assess the business role model because online marketing is growing and has effectively given a new face to advertising, public relations and branding. As suggested by Laurane Watteca, a Belgian-based graduate student in in her Youtube investigation for her final project called *"Blog mode: du succès à la derive"* ('Fashion blog: from success to drift') the typical targeted readership for these platforms is female aged 18-40.

I would add that the followers are likely to be urban or inspired by a big city lifestyle. Because of this age group, mainly Generation Y

---

202. Definition from Investopedia available from: http://www.investopedia.com/terms/p/product-life-cycle.asp
203. Ansoff, *Corporate Strategy* (1957-1965).

(and sometimes X and definitively Z), the blog needs to be updated three or four times a week as a minimum. What do we call generation X, Y and Z? Originally the term was used by Americans, William Strauss and Neil Howe (2000)[204] in their book dedicated to this early 21st Century generation of people born at the end of the post-industrial era and the beginning of the information age. This concept of having each generation characterised by social and ideological changes is helpful when it comes to understanding business development among online organisations and individuals. Generation X is defined as people belonging or sharing certain patterns in their lives including:

- Born around 1966-1976
- Age in 2016: 40-50
- High exposure to divorce and children in day care
- Highly educated[205]
- Mainly in Western countries

Generation Y (also known as "Millenials") is specified by:
- Born around 1977-1994
- Age in 2016: 22-39
- Extremely technology-driven
- Insensitive to traditional marketing campaigns as they grew up with television
- Addicted to the Internet
- Global
- Owning credit cards from an early age

Finally Generation Z: there is not much information about them as most of the people in this group are still in the process of growing

---

204. William Strauss, Neil Howe (2000) Millennials Rising: The Next Great Generation.
205. Source: Generations X,Y, Z and the Others – Cont'd, William J. Schroer.

up. However, I made an attempt to list a few main characteristics observed among teenagers and blog followers:

- Born around 1995-2012
- Age in 2015: 3-20
- Educated using brand new technology
- Addicted to fast fashion, fast food, fast information
- Almost no interest in traditional sources of information including books, television, cinema…

Interestingly these three generations are actually the core Internet users and blog followers. Whether for professional use, educational purposes, recreational activities or communication needs, Generations X, Y and Z are demanding and seeking more content online from any source in any quality or by any delivery method. Marketing companies or companies using marketing strategies to attract more consumers are aware of these three age groups who are the first in being "fully" trained in the use of the Internet as a mass medium. Furthermore, globalization in this early 21st century has accelerated the urge for new role models, stars and inspirational characters for this form of media too. The need for an online stardom (more online celebrities?) or an online élite is needed. In his book "Elites and Society"[206], Bottomore describes precisely what, where and how the meaning of the word "élite" has changed and now refers to social groups. There are two different types of élite: a ruling or governing one and a non-ruling one. Stardom has the attributes of elitism. However, as we saw in the previous chapter, stardom means recognition in all the media and sometimes also in real life. We do not know yet to what extent bloggers (also referred to as micro-celebrities or "blogebrities") will ever attain an equal status online and offline. We could nevertheless consider that the online stardom of some of the people most followed people on social media suggests that there is an online ruling elite. Successful bloggers are part of it. They know each other and sometimes befriend each other

---

206. T.B. Bottomore (1964) p. 7 -23.

sharing tips and contacts to help each other. Thus, we have observed some of the trends in business development which could be considered when identifying the strategies used to make a blog successful, bankable and attractive to viewers, advertisers and researchers. Some of the similarities we observe among successful top "White European" female bloggers are:

• Multilingual or tending to translate and post in a European language as well as English after three years of successful growth

• Introduced to lifestyle topics through the use of product placement and travel

• Desiring to develop more band association with mainstream fashion, lifestyle or beauty and health magazines

• Aiming at celebrity or fame

• Systematic about earning an income

These steps are typically referred to as market development. Market development is the strategy to promote similar products or services to people in an area which is different from where we are based. I have identified four types of market development including: new geographical markets, new product dimensions or packaging, new distribution channels and finally new market segments with differential pricing. The first and third of these are the most popular among Black bloggers. In other words, it is about blogging for people who are different from those for whom we were initially blogging. This trend is well known among mainstream bloggers. Once they have mastered their own country or the sphere of influence of their language (British bloggers can potentially reach any English-speaking reader), some bloggers decide to translate their post into another dominant language to extend their influence, grow their market and move to another level in terms of business.

The introduction to lifestyle products such as food, travel, career management tips or interior design are also typical ways of expanding a market among the viewers in their original market. If people are more interested in beauty than food, the creation of food content alongside beauty content will enable the reader to remain few more minutes on the blog. Sometimes, we can also see some of these bloggers "inviting" guests to write or talk (in an interview) about a lifestyle or specific subject that might be of interest to a large group of potential Internet users. Interaction often occurs during and after these interventions and that is exactly what they are set to achieve. The constant association with mainstream magazines or VIP events is primarily to create the uniqueness and the stardom status around the bloggers connecting with these "big names". Because the blogger is associated with "big names" she may be perceived as a "big name" herself, thus emphasizing her influence on her readers. The other aspect of this brand association will be to "touch" offline potential followers (typically people out of the Internet sphere or less connected for various reasons). Often these collaborations end up in an interview, or less often a magazine cover for the blogger and a lot of social media attention for the magazine or event which "invited" the "top blogger".

Finally, earning an income from successful blogs is crucial for the understanding of these business models. Yes, they blog because they like it and enjoy the challenge of keeping people's attention in their diaries. Yes, they are also doing it for the financial rewards, as long hours of work on a daily basis have to be paid for. Are not they entertaining people with their exceptional lives? We will not name any bloggers here as these top bloggers can easily be monitored. When it comes to top Black bloggers, I have observed a slightly different pattern in terms of business development strategies. Some Black bloggers act as their peers in the USA or notably in France but in general another set of tactics has to be used when dealing with a Black readership. Here are below some of the current techniques that I have detected:

• Penetrating the fashion sphere

• If unsuccessful in beauty or fashion blogging then lifestyle becomes a third choice

• Search for an income or creating a profitable service or product

- Desire for celebrity or fame as a main outcome of blogging
- Access to media professions becomes easier

Market penetration is a business strategy defined as techniques to expand market share. Market penetration means reaching the largest number of people in a specified target. This strategy can be sub-divided into four categories: leading the growth of the market, removing competitors, maintaining or increasing market share and finally increasing customer usage. In this instance, market penetration refers to the penetration rate and the penetration share. For the Black readership of Black blogs, this could mean getting potentially all the Black female readership in Europe to acknowledge the presence of A, B and C who own successful blogs. Event creation and development is favoured by both French and Swiss beauty bloggers while the birth of fashion collections, beauty brands or magazines are likely to seduce Black British and Black Italian lifestyle bloggers.[207] This strategy leads to several tactics including the ones we cited above. In both cases successful Black and White European bloggers seek celebrity status and money making options for their brand.

Why should we identify Black bloggers' business strategies as market penetration but for White bloggers call it market development? While most of the top white European bloggers are likely to start as a fashion or beauty or lifestyle bloggers, at least for the first three years, Black bloggers are likely to go for beauty blogging in the beginning for all the reasons we explained in the previous chapters. As a consequence, adding fashion content into beauty blogging is a must when playing in the elite blogosphere in Europe as three out of four famous Western fashion weeks occur in London, Paris and Milan. Not being visibly involved or not being visible for some top bloggers would be perceived as missing a "not to be missed" event happening only twice a year. Penetrating the fashion sphere is also about getting the attention of potential advertisers, employers and collaborators who might look for online solutions to market their

---

207. Source: surveys from C.Kedi to the 21 Black European bloggers.

companies. Being at the right place in the right time is paying off for some Black bloggers.

When penetrating the fashion sphere does not work then lifestyle, including specifically travel, is the other option that some thriving Black bloggers may choose to maintain the "VIP" factor. Travelling to… Africa! This is a strategy that may pay off well as travel is still a challenge for the most people reading online platforms. It takes time, money, organisational skills, culture, adaptation and networking skills to make it a pleasant journey. Reading what others have achieved or seen through videos or photographs is agreeable to many Black viewers. It may also inspire them to think about their next trip. For top bloggers it is doubly beneficial: keeping the crowd of followers interested and attracting potential sponsors or readers from different places attracted by the new content.

Black bloggers based in Africa or the Caribbean may experience some administrative challenges which limit the potential expansion of their network and their reach to a local readership. Similarly, Black American bloggers hardly ever travel outside of the USA since their principle readership, and probably their main target, is American. This partly explains the phenomenon of the Black European blogger enjoying the travel option as a major aspect of lifestyle.

In the first chapters we assessed the hierarchy of Black influence in the Black world and how Black European bloggers were initially influenced by African Americans. However, when they do not receive as much feedback or reward because the scale of the market which is different in Europe and where the Black population is much more diverse than in the USA, they tend to go back into their "Afropolitanity" to increase their visibility and viewership and eventually their influence. The search for financial reward is obviously a must for all top bloggers. Countless brand associations, advertisements for manufacturers of products or services and many more practices aim to make the online platform bankable. This is not a critique but a reward for hours of unpaid work prior to becoming a successful blogger.

Now the final aspect which is interesting for Black bloggers when compared to their White peers is that they have easier access to the professions because of their visibility. Blogging, as we explained earlier, was used (and still is) differently by Western and African people. Convenient and competitively priced, online media offer a source of information that a majority of people can access without the burden of a TV licence or electricity bill. Internet cafés in Africa are everywhere and not too expensive to use. As television is costly to maintain and is challenged by online TV, the Internet offers the pleasure of being alone in front of a screen enjoying programmes and readings of one's choice at any time of the day, anywhere in the world. This has seduced countless African media structures who have adopted the Internet as their principal marketing tool and later as a medium on its own. Being "visible" online for an African community still means "being credible". Credibility is partly built on geography, Black hierarchy of influence and constant updates and undisputed content generation. Perceived as they present themselves online, top Black European bloggers are attractive to Black media to support their quest to conquer online markets. Some are booked for advice on Internet solutions, social media development strategy or online marketing. All these areas require specific expertise gained after intensive training that few could justify. After all, the fact of being online, if it attracts people, is a way of showing the blogger's competence in a given area!

3. Strategically making money legally

Business development strategy also implies making money legally. As previously described, when placing Black culture as a business model it is, according to Dr Dalphinis,[208] necessary to comply with the need to become a successful business manager. To him, Black managers experience similar challenges to their White peers but also additional ones that make leadership and application of management

---

208. Black people and management (2015) p. 17-26.

techniques more challenging than for any other group of leaders. Dr Dalphinis maintains that the use of traditional tools such as SWOT and Ansoff matrix to understand the type of business management is incomplete when considering Black entrepreneurship. He adds to the list STEP (see below), the cultural web, leadership and management competence.

What Dr Dalphinis calls STEP (here adapted to the African continent) is:

• Social instability (in Africa: wars, societies in crisis leading to chronic dysfunctional systems)

• Technological dependency on other nations outside Africa's cultural sphere of influence

• Economic challenges for the average citizen

• Personal policy management driven by self-optimisation

All these questions may explain why a Black manager dealing with a Black readership may have an impact on how to deal with people originating from these areas. How the branding of the African continent may lead to the disparagement of or lack of trust in any African in a situation of power since they perceived as being weak at long term planning.

Secondly, let us observe what Dr Dalphinis calls the cultural web applied to an African context:

• Rituals and myths are spiritual while for Western societies they may be materialistic: becoming an adult could be associated with being independent, perhaps owning and driving a car. In an African context the rite of passage may be more symbolic.

• Lifestyle symbols: big TV screens are symbolic among Africans (especially those living in Europe or North America) of reaching a certain level of comfort; while for a European, having more holidays may indicate a more comfortable lifestyle.

• Weak control systems and naivety: any blogger can claim to be an online marketing specialist in an African community while Europeans may be more cautious.

• Hierarchy is important within Black organisations. Africans have inherited this from traditional societies and from the colonial class system and are now facing a double social stigma whether they are in Africa or outside. European societies depend more on legitimacy and still to some extent elitism.

• Powers are inherited from others. African governance is a pale copy of what the colonialists left. European governance is challenged by lobbies, civil society, multinational companies, and even individual citizens.

What does this mean for Black bloggers? They need to constantly reassess the needs of their readers to evaluate the impact of their content on people. They should ideally try to become as independent as possible: dependency on others' technology, finance and cultural references is risky for a business. Constant outsourcing of resources can kill a business. Thus, the participatory nature of blogging creates a conversation among Blacks and ethnic minorities in general. It also underlines the reality of corporate appropriation of the Internet through the sales on platforms such as Wordpress or Tumblr.

Leadership should be modified to cater for this demanding group. Dr Dalphinis emphasises several types of Black British management[209] which I have assessed against the nature of Black blogging for a female readership in Europe as well as the very personal nature of online business based on personal branding. This can be characterised as:

• Blacklist
• Coconut
• Developmental

Blacklist refers to the "extremist movement" called "Nappy" which I have chosen to illustrate this trend in management which we can find all across Europe. "Black hair is better" is the psychology behind this. Often based upon a certain reading of Black activism (often

---

209. Dalphinis, M (1997) New controversial discussions for British Institute of Integrative Psychotherapy.

African-American activism), these bloggers do not acknowledge the variety within the African identity: skin colour is the principal sign of recognition. They see racism as a consequence of pure evil and motivated by hate. Racism justifies a certain type of radicalised leadership. Born out of centuries of trauma, Blacklist is racially motivated: the only leaders are Black.

Coconut refers to typical blogs which are trying to "reach out each and everyone, not only Black people" since their perception is that "being too black" or "writing and blogging officially for Blacks" is offensive. Here racism is usually perceived as a normal phenomenon among humans. These are the typical bloggers who would ignore statistics about multinational companies who hardly ever hire Blacks but who sponsor them on their blog from time to time. These bloggers also share views about "adapting" to Western societies as an assimilation process. They will claim that they are mixed in their identities: Afropean, Afropolitan…anything but African. Their leaders can be anyone who does not claim to be an African national.

Developmental refers to the typical cultural activist blogger or the organised lobby. Acknowledging international standards, identifying policies and actions that are bad for the entire community and specifically to the blogger. These bloggers often work in groups. They collaborate with local organisations and professionals to gain credibility as citizens and communicate with governing authorities. Racism is perceived as a collective pain. The preferred leadership is about having the best representation without being perceived as victims.

In all these examples of Black leadership among bloggers, we see that most of these options are motivated by recent history and long term trauma fed by Americanised perceptions. To find the best balance for Black management of online platforms, competencies needed to develop a culturally charged approach should encompass:

• The management of anti-oppressive practices here symbolised by the "Blacklist" or so called "Nappys"

• The assessment of learning through experience – autobiography and other forms of narrative. This would lead to the management of knowledge among bloggers and vloggers.

• The historical evaluation of the principles of cultural resistance among lobbyists. How to comply and cope with constant changes in the law? How to inform without acting like victims or "Blacklist"?

Making money legally is central to all these principles of Black management, leadership and cultural self-understanding. Once a blogger has fully highlighted the areas to develop as a potential "influencer", maintaining the content and sharing of information will be unlimited and he or she will need to rely on other ways to raise income. This may badly affect the blogger's initial desire to inform. How do Black bloggers make money? As with other bloggers, the number of followers is vital to manufacturers and global companies who will approach them for deals. The more bloggers have a relatively constant viewership on Google analytics, the better and faster they will be contacted for product endorsement and placement. Keen in his 2007 publication defined the phenomenon as: "a propaganda instrument, a marketing tool and a distribution channel." For the reasons we explored in the first chapters, Black bloggers are not always perceived as fashion icons. One impact of this reality is the limited number of fashion and lifestyle deals offered to leading Black bloggers. The beauty industry is more considerate about this ethnic group, since according to several reports including Datamonitor and Marketline,[210] Black women are the female ethnic group spending the most in Western countries when it comes to hair and beauty products. Knowing this, manufacturers are interested in making sure it continues by getting through to young people from generation Z at an early age.

As bloggers are aware of their target in terms of their age group, location, origin and occupation they accordingly adapt and adopt the codes emulated by these followers. Some typical examples can be evaluated according to the type of comments left on bloggers' platforms. Many of these readers do not hesitate to use their real names, where they live, sometimes their age (depending on the culture) and their profession. If asked about hair care for busy working mothers,

---

210. Beautifying the Body in Ancient Africa and today (2013) C. Kedi.

the blogger may guess the respondent's age group and propose a tailor-made solution by offering a one to one session. Private consultations have been booming in Afro hair care over the last decade. There are almost no bloggers who are not themselves proposing (sometimes through partnership) hair care services on site, at home or online. Whatever the deal, the consumer is still entitled to pay for the offer. Lately during one of the numerous conversations I have had with bloggers, it was revealed that some of them were offering "blogging consultations". These are one to one appointments sold in series to young and aspiring bloggers who would like to understand the mysteries and secrets of becoming a "top" blogger. Private sessions are common while group work is considered as a protection among bloggers to "preserve" their market of potential customers booking appointments at hairdressers! Making money is not for all bloggers. It is an extra. This extra should be animated by the desire to transform a demanding hobby into a full time career. A career of entrepreneurship also entails commitments, discipline, finance management, taking risks, decision-making skills, strategy and marketing. Not everyone is made for business!

There are several ways of generating income online. For the purpose of this section I would divide these tools into four categories: sponsored contents; advertising; consultancy; and working with agencies.

Sponsored contents include product placement, sponsored articles or sponsored travel. The blogger would receive products, services or financial rewards (or all three) – in return for writing, mentioning or wearing the product, service, travel, event or book and describing it. This form of income is the most obvious in the blogosphere. In a recent video on Youtube Laurane Watteca mentioned getting paid hundreds of euros for featuring once on her blog about 200-300 words about a product she tested. According to European law[211], these practices are legal if the blogger mentions the sponsoring of the feature

---

211. EU Directive May 2005.

so that the consumer is fully aware that the content has been paid for and does not just represent the views of the blogger. Not complying with these laws may lead to a nearly €40,000 fine. It is unfortunately common practice for some bloggers not to mention they have been paid (even in kind) to "share their findings" about the product. In the beauty industry and travel blogging, this is common and too often unnoticed by the readers. "Clogs" and "flogs" are sub-categories of sponsored content, designated by Deuze in his 2007 research article entitled: "Ethnic media, community media and participatory culture." The clogs are the abbreviations of the words "corporate" and "blog". They are used as marketing tools by some corporations in need of specific online presence in order to target a certain type of people.

The advertisement is the second way for bloggers to make money. It is simple and easy. Once the blogger has reached 100,000 followers on different social media, they are likely to be approached by multi-nationals, search engines and PR/marketing companies who are willing to pay to get an advertisement in the right corner or on the bottom of the blog. Now some also add a link which redirects to their website, enabling the viewer to buy online. In that case these bloggers can also be paid by clicking and can gain a percentage for each purchase from their followers.

Consultancy. During my investigation, I recently learned that some bloggers are selling their "knowledge" to aspiring bloggers, marketing departments of companies or beauty, fashion or lifestyle brands. Paid hourly or after the completion of a contract, these "consultancies" may become extremely lucrative especially when the blogger has to deliver a medium to long term project (over three months). Collaborations are typically in that category.

Working with agencies. Finally, I have chosen to focus on "talent management agencies", though there are several other ways to make a blog financially viable. Why talent agencies? Because this growing phenomenon has reached the Black blogosphere in Europe, creating even more potential careers in blogging due to the nature of the work they do. Top bloggers are joining agencies who are exclusively dealing with people "in demand" and with "rising profiles". Since bloggers have to focus on content generation all day, managing some aspect of their business lives might still be challenging for these micro-enterprises. Therefore, talent agencies are responsible for finding the best deals for their clients. These can include advertisements, sponsored content, consultancy, modelling, TV presentation, events, acting, dancing, singing, writing and literally whatever the demand is for as long as the clients can pay the price. Many articles, websites and books have focused on how money can be made online, always claiming it is easy. In regard to the legal side of the business, money making can face several challenges. One is copyright: some Black bloggers are known for attending conferences and recording the content to "rewrite it" as their own. I have unfortunately had to witness this. Another is infringement of the law. I have heard of bloggers not registering their taxes, online income or business structures to the authorities while their sponsors declared that they had them from their marketing budget.

Due to competition among beauty, fashion and lifestyle journalists, some bloggers assume titles including those of fashion or beauty editors when joining media companies. They should ensure that these titles are linked to their qualifications and experience in these professions. The Black blogosphere, as well as organising business growth has also to manage its followers and then keep happy. Imagery is vital.

4. Visual branding: trends in web design

As in areas of design, web design is also subject to waves or trends. Bloggers are often admired for the quality of visual content they share with their readers. Photography is one of the main aspects of the process but nevertheless a beautiful picture posted on an average looking blog may not be noticed. The layout, the functionality, the background and the feel were all suggested in our personal investigation into the world of online content. In fact, I managed to find some relatively consistent features in the appearance and presentation of top blogs. The reason why visual branding and trends in web design are included alongside business strategies and not in a different chapter is obvious: blogs are selling images, often videos (also known as video-blogs or vlogs), sometimes sounds (in this case they are called audio-blogs) and perhaps on mobile phones (also known as mobile-blogs or mblogs). The more a blogger grows in terms of influence the more the website will reflect the changes happening in the business life of its author.

WHO DOES BLOG?

Who blogs in Black Europe? (C. Kedi, 2015)

As seen in the schema above, there are different types of bloggers and as we saw in an earlier chapter there are different forms of blogging too. Bloggers are usually divided into different categories according to the type of profile they choose to create. Here I chose to focus on eight categories of bloggers based on the results of my assessment. Accordingly their branding strategies and use of Internet will give information about the way in which they try to maintain viewership. Freelancers were not added to the schema since most of the top bloggers are in fact freelance either as self-employed, as a registered business or as the sole decision maker on their online platform. Depending on the viewership they want to attract, the choice of a platform may change. Some of the people who took part in the survey were trained in art, others were marketing graduates and few had a business or media background. This initial training had a huge impact on how they present their online platforms. Despite the few who were actually niche experts or professionals from the fashion scene, the majority were not and were likely to join the category of business owner, platform builder product promoter or professional blogger.

A few bloggers combined two or more of the eight types. For example, one blogger was a fashion professional, a post-graduate in a fashion related subject, who built a platform to promote her designs while organising conferences and events for niche experts and fellow fashion professionals. Another example would be a business owner who owns an online platform selling products. She uses her skills to appear as a professional blogger to set up events where beauty professionals who sell their products through her online platform can act as niche experts by providing content to her readers. More examples will be displayed in the last part of this book. Below are the general rules that I found during the observation period of my investigation.

- White background was largely preferred to any other colour.
- Wordpress is often the preferred web software.
- Photography is used more than other forms of graphics.
- There should be as few written words as possible.

- Links to all social media are required.
- No geographical location should be shown.
- Collaborations with individuals should be fully credited.
- Email addresses are available but rarely phone numbers.
- Use of sounds and moving images should be limited.

These features can be explained according to the type of followers. Generation Y and Z as demonstrated earlier are unlikely to read posts of more than 800 words. They are unlikely to read the posts if images are not added to the text. The same generations are likely to be more sensitive to photography than graphic art as illustrations. For the blogger, photography is also competitively priced in comparison to hiring an artist to design for a viewership that has little interest in graphic arts (unless related to some "Afropolitan" themes such as the over-used Adinkra alphabet). The email addresses are there to avoid unsolicited and excessive demands from people who are keen on getting more information for free.

The use of the Wordpress platform is likely to be preferred as it enables mobile blogging with control over the comments posted on the blog. Easy management of the platform is also one of the main features that a majority of bloggers admitted they took into account when they chose to invest in a Wordpress type of template, (Gabriel, 2014). Wordpress also allows a large choice of colours and themes grouped according to specific needs: portfolio blog, business blog, article blog. The freedom of changing the design with just one little click is also offered by competitors but with less variety of choices. The use of the white background for the entire blog is associated with the practice of feeding blogs with photography: pictures stand out well against white backgrounds. White backgrounds are also used by "high end" online platforms for established fashion magazines. Black backgrounds are sometimes used by professionals such as photographers to give a feeling of authority in using this visual art form. What we also realised was appealing in terms of web design selection was the way in which the elements of the design could be transformed over time. We observed some of these bloggers from an early age and witnessed the rapid changes that have occurred on their platforms for a better online experience. Among the most evident were:

- Trying to be brief and succinct.
- Choosing a font which highlights the most valuable contents and titles, including goodies and offers to readers.
- Having good quality photographs.
- Diversification of the content.
- Consistency in updates and posts.

All these elements make the blog stand out of the crowd and therefore creates a need for the first time reader to come back. In the meantime, there is a technical aspect to consider when analysing the trends in web design.

- Scalable vector graphics
- Interaction
- Ghost buttons
- Mobile blogging

Scalable vector graphics are two dimensional types of graphics which give a certain type of appearance on a blog or online platform. They are among the strong upcoming trends at the present time according to Web Design Wall[212] as they provide a lively feeling to a website creating a sophisticated image often mixed with photography. Seen on most of the luxury brands' online sites, they show that the entire fashion industry will follow what was already used in the beauty industry. These SVGs are an opening door to a moving a vlog.

Interaction is also a strong and long term strategy used in web design among bloggers. The principle of blogging is to share opinions and content and therefore blogs must interact, grow and be maintained according to the constant demands. In that context,

---

212. Reference available from: http:// webdesignerwall.com/trends/7-web-design-trends-to-watch-for-in-2015

the Mblogging (Mobile blogging) has seen many blogs reorganising their data to fit tablets and mobile phones for a continuous opinion sharing experience. The interaction has been improved by the device developers who know allow applications to be shared on one's entire internet-connected devices. Ghost buttons are finally the last strong emerging trend in web design that we have so far witnessed among the bloggers approached. Originally provided by the hosting plat-forms as optional, with years they have become compulsory. Stylish and discreet, the ghost buttons blend into the general feel and back-ground of the website. As a consequence, they are a safe option when a blog has been on for over five years since they support the data management of daily posts without a need to compromise the actual design. In other words, the ghost buttons enable a blogger to manage with more autonomy and efficiency hold posts from previous years without having to delete, hide or expose the entire stock of posts.

Part III

Case studies and portraits

Chapter VI
Afropolitan trends

1. Fashion promotion: Case study

In this last part, we will evaluate through real life case studies how some blogs may find common ground and lay the foundations for entrepreneurship in the best possible conditions. Respecting the legal framework, business ethics, developing educative content using entertaining tools can make a difference to how beauty and fashion professionals may interfere with bloggers. This may also influence the way readers get information from a consumer perspective without necessarily having to join the crowd of lobbyists. In the first example, we will assess how ethical African fashion can be made widely available to both the professional and general public according to the standards of the industry in terms of sourcing the information, diffusing it and interacting with the readership. To do so we have chosen a British website registered as a social enterprise and created by a fashion professional with international experience. The aim of this online platform is to inform ethical practices in Africa while placing them into an international context for a better competitive experience and growth. When exploring the history of ethical brands in the UK, these issues have been influencing consumer behaviour since as early as the 70s. Following the burgeoning of the anti-consumerism movement, British society has greatly contributed to the launch of several global organisations aiming at protecting nature. Campaigns for animal protection and rights and denouncing the impact of deforestation have eventually led to the development of a growing demand for corporate responsibility. Consequently, marketing policies to address these issues have targeted first the food chain and later the fashion industry. However, the fashion industry took years to analyse such practices. It should have acknowledged both the ecological and human factors involved in the numerous processes of garment creation and production. By comparison, the beauty industry was from early on concerned with unethical practices, probably due to the direct relationship that cosmetics have with the human body.

The main challenges that have affected the ethical fashion brands in reaching the average consumer more effectively seem to result from a lack of association between clothing the body and ethical production of fabrics and from a misunderstanding of the supply and value chains. Initially based on visual semiotics alongside branding strategies borrowed from the mainstream fashion industry, ethical fashion took longer to acknowledge the unforeseen results of embarrassing practices to reach a mass market. Therefore, ethical fashion in the collective mind is still perceived and identified with a subculture while ethical beauty is not. Branding is at the heart of our understanding of how clothes and nature are linked to us. The past decade has seen the rapid development of sustainability and ethical responsibility in many fashion and beauty related topics leading to the improvement of ethical brands in terms of visibility. However, these rapid changes are having a serious effect on the purchaser's behaviour: "A third of consumers are prepared to consider green factors when purchasing clothing or accessories [...]" "the greening of fashion industry".[213] While ethical beauty in the UK has developed alongside an educational movement about the environmental and health factors involved in the production of inexpensive fast beauty products, "clothing retailers have been focusing more on sustainable fashion, with a growing trend for recycling initiatives."[214] In all cases, progress in consumers' behaviour has been witnessed: "the ethical impact". In initiatives such as the African Fashion Guide online platform, the ethical expert and fashion designer Jacqueline Shaw had

213. Mintel, 2008.
214. Mintel, 2008

to answer a constantly growing demand to promote sustainability practices in African fashion markets.

Africa Fashion Guide online promotional image. Picture by A. Oshodi

She chose to disseminate knowledge using available technology and her experience in creating and making clothes herself to share opinions and information about *ecofashion* in the Black and African sphere. Ecofashion, like Afropolitanism, is a means of self-perception within a Western environment. Jacqueline has chosen to re-create the original connection existing between the southern hemisphere and fashion on the one hand and "Africanness", diaspora and trend consumerism on the other. How did she make it? She trained herself. She travelled extensively. She wrote up her projects. She reflected and created thoughts and joined the dots. She researched. In a few words, the development of her initiative was also a combination of her own experiences and views about citizenship, identity, knowledge of the industry and the globalization of trends. Her cultural web was re-assessed to serve the purpose of her project. Her project was to improve the image the fashion industry from different perspectives. Linking consumerism to knowledge of the industry to make for a better practice was the idea. The use of a web-based platform was also a consequence of having:

- a democratic communication tool
- a visually attractive experience
- an interactive project
- a professional tool

To date various methods have been developed and introduced to measure ethically orientated educational tools including seminars, workshops and training days. Nevertheless a competitively priced approach was chosen by Jacqueline because of its consequences for individuals' perceptions on the subject. Ecofashion, Afropolitanism and global warming are still considered by many as "hipster" culture, a sub-culture only available to those who are less challenged by the everyday need to pay bills and buy affordable clothes. In this case study Jacqueline had to identify fashion imaging and eco-orientated creative story lines to promote campaigns related to African ethical fashion. She also had to find an easily presentable way to promote knowledge about the value chain, production channels and working practices for a workforce living in the southern hemisphere. Jacqueline had to face the absence of "sexiness" in the ecofashion debate. She was able to overcome the lack of interest from the Black community for a fashion system outside of its imagery, glamour and culture thanks to her expertise and inside knowledge. Similarly, the case study was chosen to offer a qualitative and comprehensive interpretative view on a specific subject: the promotion of fashion. However, there are certain challenges associated with the use of both focus groups and case studies: time management; ethics (participants may not be interested in being identified on recording material); and limitations in the observation and interpretation of the results (the examples may turn out to be exceptions). For this case study, the choice of brands was used to assess the impact of branding on a consumer sample of ethical brands. Two emerging brands were selected with less than five years business activity: one an ethical beauty company, *Raw Skin Food;* the other an ethical fashion company, *Sapelle*.

To promote both beauty and fashion there is a need to identify online strategies used by professionals in the dissemination of a niche trend for ethical products and/or services in order to validate the role that social media and networks now play. That need was the ultimate goal of this case study. The methodologies used were a mixture of website observation and document analysis. This was performed using logos and online research. Each brand's Facebook page and first online page were analysed. The interviews related to the two brands were conducted informally by email. Investigations of fashion promotion using online tools are still rare. In these case studies, attention has been paid to the visual semiotics, specifically logos and websites. To enable the target subjects to see logos and websites clearly, as the room did not possess a large screen, the images were projected onto plain white paper. The initial sample consisted of several adults, an equal representation of women and men aged 18 to 35 years old. The choice was to run this focus group in a south London health and lifestyle store offering free awareness workshops on Saturday evenings. The chosen sample (students and new professionals C1 and C2) was perceived as being the most likely (60%) to make a use of online platforms to identify and buy ethical products. A small sample was chosen because

Africa Fashion Guide online promotional image. Picture by A. Oshodi

of the expected difficulty of obtaining release forms and time to evaluate the findings. The focus group lasted 20 minutes and the subjects had to read and answer the questions in writing. The findings were to focus on the two emerging brands as they captured more attention during focus group. The first set of analyses examined the impact of female consumers and their knowledge on how to source ethical brands. From the answers given by both *Raw Skin Food* and *Sapelle*, both brands were well aware of their local UK market demands as well as their international customer base. In both cases the heavily female orientated database of clients is mentioned: ranging from 25 to 50 for *Sapelle* and from 25 to 75 for *Raw Skin Food*. *Sapelle* also describes the Internet as; "very helpful, our best means of communicating to our target audience." The most striking result to emerge from the data is that *Sapelle* has 1,647 Facebook followers which confirms *Sapelle's* need to rely on online shopping habits.

Nevertheless several factors meanwhile have created awareness and confusion: *ecofashion*, fair trade, natural and organic are terms nowadays often associated with brands and logos and sometimes green certification. Retro, vintage, second hand and homemade beauty products have increased interest ethics when dressing the body. As mentioned by Dafydd Beard (2008)[215]: "Indeed, for the consumer, "vintage" and "ethical" are seemingly synonymous". Despite the Rana Plaza disaster in Bangladesh on 24 April 2013, there has been little agreement on how the ethical fashion scene could organise itself more honestly online. Debate continues about the best strategies for the management of eco-shopping: the Internet is leading the field for eco brands. Our findings suggest that both the *Africa Fashion Guide* and *Sapelle* are using the Internet to raise awareness among consumers. These two examples show creative ways of blogging for a targeted readership. Professionally trained, these two brands have made the extra effort to approach others to support their work: graphic designers, writers, fashion stylists and photographers have all participated in these projects. Creativity and business can work alongside ethics in business, life and fashion!

---

215. The Branding of Ethical Fashion and the Consumer: A Luxury Niche or Mass-market Reality?

2. Beauty promotion: Case study

Raw Skin Food indicated that the recession hit ethical beauty brands due to lack of information from customers about the quality of products. The supply/value underlined the remarks from Mintel in February 2013: "Low levels of regulation have not helped the natural and organics industry, [...] meant that manufacturers have been able to exploit the label, leading to widespread distrust and confusion among consumers." For *Raw Skin Food*: "[...] a growing amount of information on general websites [...] is very contradictory and not correct scientifically [...]". For Dafydd Beard[216]: "[...] As eco-orientated cosmetic firms [...] the best way to inform people about your product is to encourage them to try it out [...]. For S: "online customers shop because they are seeking the African trend [...] very few [...] express an interest that's driven by ethical consideration". Turning now to the evidence from focus groups, 3 out 4 fully answered the questions stating that for 50% were attracted by the spiritual side of the latest logo by *Raw Skin Food*, "Free your mind". Some of the subjects even suggested changing its colour to blue for more appealing results. In all cases, *Raw Skin Food's* website and logo stood out more than the three others. This finding corroborates the ideas of Breward who suggests that: "the relationship between production, consumption, and the designed object [...] demands an investigation of context [...] of historical and contemporary clothing". The results of this case study indicate that branding serves to communicate social and historical commitments. Images and perceptions are socially composed. "A company's corporate image is fundamental to its long-term wellbeing, [...] to attract sales [...] reliable staff. [...] A good corporate image means consumers are more likely to give the company the benefit [...]". These findings further support Breward's idea on visual symbols: "the expression of form in the simplest of terms [...] is particularly necessary in fashion drawing". This experiment did not detect any evidence of a lack of interest in the visual

---

216. Dafydd Beard (2008)

imagery presented to the subject who answered. *Sapelle* had a black and white logo with visual imagery on its website's first page.

For the fashion theorist, when linking these details to the history of UK fashion and its promotion: "one important lesson to be gained from the study of fashion promotion and diffusion [...] is the realisation of their power [...] in suggesting, reflecting and sustaining lifestyles". Ethical beauty brands are learning from their customers at the same time as they seem to offer ethical knowledge about skin care. There are several possible explanations for these results. A possible explanation may be the lack of an adequate: "clear and simple message that is tangible and exciting, yet devoid of confusing jargon [...]". Visual imagery with a selected language of colours as suggested by one of the members of the focus group should be able to create an identity for ethical brands. Contrary to expectations, this case study did not find a significant difference between the visual images of the ethical brands: only the colours seemed to have attracted the attention of the focus group. In the UK, the importance of regularly rebranding logos for ethical beauty companies such as *Raw Skin Food* does seem to support the online promotion of these brands by increasing the memory of the consumer who had already used the products. The status of ethical fashion brands is equally efficient if they develop customers' awareness by educating them. Findings suggest there is a large potential pool of consumers who are ready to buy ethical if the conditions are right.[217] Therefore, if the Black Blogosphere is willing to promote fashion and beauty using sustainability as a focus point it has to consider the impact of visual imagery on online consumerism. The African Fashion Guide has done it and is therefore regarded as a promotional and educational platform on the subject. Too few Black online platforms in Europe seem to understand the realities of being simultaneously in two sub-cultures – as a minority group promoting the sometimes misunderstood values of *ecofashio*n.

---

217. Mintel, February 2013.

3. Lifestyle promotion: Case study

Afropolitan trends in necklaces over the last three years have greatly influenced the African and Caribbean orientated boutiques located in London, Paris and Milan. In this case study, we purposely selected four boutiques in South and East London. These areas have a significant African presence and therefore consumer interest in African products and culture. Sonia Ashmore[218] mentioned: "The emergence of exotic dress styles in retain during the 1960s and early 1970s, was neither a designer-led phenomenon, nor quite a "street style", but a form of counter-cultural expression that arrived through less predictable routes and cultural milieu." This trend has forged and developed a network of lifestyle and fashion boutiques dedicated to the promotion of cosmo-politanism and democratic channels of dissemination of trends through the Internet and word of mouth. Initially targeting the Bohemian and trendy crowds all over Europe, "Afropolitan" necklaces have now hit both mainstream and High Street stores in UK. These trends seemed to have originated from some areas of London where boutiques acted as trendsetters. To evaluate how some of these African-orientated boutiques may have been involved, the examination of recent styles between 2011 and 2014 was analysed against the fashion theories related to the crea-tion of trends, the concept of fashion cities and its relation with fashion myths and finally the power of visual merchandizing.

Primary research targeted the understanding of visual merchan-dizing, location and niche markets in areas with an African presence and therefore an initial pool of buyers for these specific styles. The visits and interviews of four boutique owners in Brixton, Shoreditch and Sydenham showed how to select specific necklaces and how to sell them to Londoners and to anyone else. Opened at different periods and with a good visual display they offered a starting point for the creation of a trend of selling African necklaces. This study iden-tified the trend in the sale of necklaces, mapped the trend in limited parts of London, recognised the similarities in the type of display among African-orientated shop owners and confirmed reports that craft necklaces are sought by Afropolitans.

---

218. Fashion's World Cities (2006).

Larache boutique (Shoreditch), picture by C. Kedi

The outcome of this case study presented as a trend report also highlighted the power of online social media when considering the dissemination of such trends, using bloggers and fashion professionals as an effective way to endorse the necklaces and where to find them. The bloggers also supported the identification of Afropolitanism, as discussed above. There was clearly a need for boutiques selling Afropolitan necklaces (and other items) to visually stimulate all types of clients.

According to Jaime Cohn-Barr from WGSN,[219] brands that create "wearable art" and craft-inspired jewellery are highlights at *Accessorie Circuit* autumn/winter 2014-15". This report mainly aims at distinguishing an Afro-Caribbean pool of buyers. This tendency can be confirmed by the observation of Afro-Caribbean orientated female online magazines over the last three years (see images above) in which the type of necklaces reflects the notion of craftsmanship by the shape, its form or the material in which they are designed.

---

219. Source: www.wgsn.com.

Pempamsie boutique (Brixton); Picture by C. Kedi

The colour range is also a determining factor: colours allow some customers to classify a necklace whether it is designed for men, women or both as suggested by one of the accessory designers Nosah, who have set up a brand of scarf made out of beads (see pictures below). Another example is the different options a shop window display may stimulate if colourful necklaces are added. To better understand the typology of the ideal buyer for some of these boutiques in London, it is important to remember the concept of Afropolitanism. Being Black British (or by extension Black European) and a Londoner is as mentioned by Berenice Geoffroy-Schneiter: "It's an Africa that (is) European, American, Caribbean, and nationalist [...]". Over the last 12 years, the growing style of European-based African fashion has blossomed due to a mixture of events, the launch of both online and off line boutiques, promotion of designers by both African stylists and photographers –and blogs. Afropolitan east Londoners such as the boutique Soboye (in Shoreditch– see picture below) were among the first trend setters in developing the idea of a Black lifestyle/fashion boutique with an exhibition type of display.

Soboye Boutique in Shoreditch (London) Picture by C. Kedi

Similarly, the Larache boutique of the renowned Moroccan photographer and artist Hassan Hajjaj is equally celebrated as one of the best African fashion spots in London. Created by the artist, the ambiance is created by displays of the latest trends in visual art.

To conclude, study of Black Europeans from a fashion perspective is about identifying who the key players are, where they create trends, why are they located in specific areas in Europe, often matching the mainstream socio-geographical trends and why they choose to transform their followers into either a buying pool of their own products and services or as a database to be sold to multinational companies using s-commerce and six Cs theories.

The next part will introduce the understanding of how they disseminate the trends and how effective their business strategies are, if they have any. The target consumer is a mixture of *Bobo* (Bohemians and Bourgeois) and middle to upper class Afro-Caribbeans for both Parisian and Milanese markets as these products are priced as luxury items, *Afropolitan* crowds, including artists, students, former hippies, naturalistas, and ethically aware costumers for the London markets and few lovers of accessories. Consequently boutiques are tailored to stimulate these consumers visually and they are located to take into account demographic changes in the cities in question. People buying Afropolitan necklaces are stimulated by the colour range as seen with three different designers over the last three years reflecting a trend set around primary colours: red, yellow and blue as seen on Anitah Quansah, Nosah Khary, Vanessa Mooney, Stella Jean or Ben Amun. In the meantime, the shapes and type of beads are likely to look handcrafted, "ethnic" or inspired by embroidery, as seen below with Frieda Luhl and Sany Huyn. In the picture above, the shop window of *Pempamsie*, a lifestyle and general interest boutique located on Brixton Hill in South London, bright colours are used as well as beads but once inside the shop, the necklaces presented are mainly made out of semi-precious materials. The colourful pieces are no longer on the central shelves.

Locations and displays offer a styling option to tempt consumers who are not sure about these bold and sometimes artistic pieces.

Necklaces by Anita Quansah and scarf by Nosakhari. Styling and picture by C. Kedi

The necklaces such as those from Anita Quansah are sometimes challenging to style for visual display and wear, while Ben Amun may offer a safer option, but his work is handcrafted since he targets larger distribution channels. The primary colours, shapes and beads have all still remained safely trendy and similar since 2011. In the meantime, the colour ranges and shapes for types of necklaces follow the trends arriving from Africa or inspired from there.

Chapter VII
Black european leading blogs: an overview

This last chapter presents of a selection of Black blogs which aim to be ethical and have been created by people who still claim to share some common lifestyle, art forms, history and ancestry. The Black blogosphere in Europe, whether dedicated to beauty, fashion or lifestyle, can be a controversial and exciting business venture. Although each online platform has its limitations, identity is still at the core of its function. However, the way it functions should satisfy the needs of its targeted followers. The readership must be kept entertained, informed and updated.

As shown below, I located these bloggers geographically and evaluated their effectiveness with regard to business options, culture dissemination, identity questions and aesthetics. The map below shows the location of the 21 bloggers who kindly collaborated by answering some basic questions about their work and achievements.

This final section includes some success stories, a selection of blogs or online platforms across Europe. These men and women are working hard to enhance the Afropolitan experience in European fashion cities and to search for the perfect layout, visuals and content. It reflects some of the common questions the bloggers answered to give some background to their work, their location and their inspiration. Some of the questions may have been answered fully, others not. This selection is not exhaustive but gives an idea of what can be done to meet the needs of both readers and business.

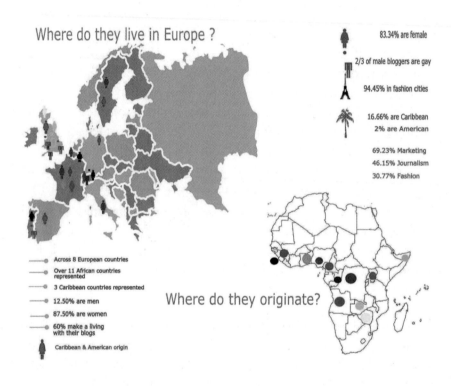

Where do they live in Europe ?

83.34% are female

2/3 of male bloggers are gay

94.45% in fashion cities

16.66% are Caribbean
2% are American

69.23% Marketing
46.15% Journalism
30.77% Fashion

Across 8 European countries
Over 11 African countries represented
3 Caribbean countries represented
12.50% are men
87.50% are women
60% make a living with their blogs
Caribbean & American origin

Where do they originate?

Portrait 1: Afroblush

AFROBLUSH

AFROPEAN FASHION | LIFESTYLE | CULTURE

Afroblush
www.afroblush.com
Uganda
Lives in United Kingdom
Launched in 2011
Few words: As a noun it's just a blog, a website, and/or blogazine. Do you mean adjectives?

Name: Afroblush

URL: www.afroblush.com

Country of origin: Uganda

Country of residence: United Kingdom

Launched: 2011

In a few words: It's just a blog, a website, and/or a blogazine

Portrait 2: Urbamen

Urbamen
www.urbamen.com
Guadeloupe
Lives in UK
Launched in 2012
Few words: -

Name: URBAMEN
URL: www.urbamen.com
Country of origin: France (Guadeloupe)
Country of residence: UK
Launched: 2012

Portrait 3: FabAfrique

FabAfrig

INSPIRE INFORM INNOVATE ENTERTAIN

FabAfrique
www.fabafrique.com
Cameroon
Lives in United Kingdom
Launched her blog 4 years ago
Few words: Lifestyle

Name: FabAfrique

URL: www.fabafrique.com

Country of origin: Cameroon

Country of residence: United Kingdom

Launched: 2010

In a few words: lifestyle

Portrait 4: Si Paris était une femme – femme en capital – (If Paris was a woman – woman in the capital)

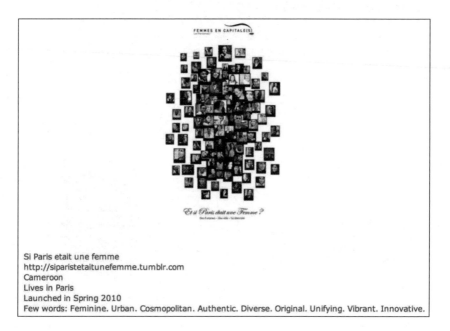

Si Paris etait une femme
http://siparistetaitunefemme.tumblr.com
Cameroon
Lives in Paris
Launched in Spring 2010
Few words: Feminine. Urban. Cosmopolitan. Authentic. Diverse. Original. Unifying. Vibrant. Innovative.

Name: Femme en capitale

URL: www.femmeencapitale.canalblog.com

Country of origin: Cameroon

Country of residence: France

Launched: Spring 2010

A few words: Feminine. Cosmopolitan. Multicultural. Authentic. Diverse. Original. Unifying. Vibrant. Innovative

Portrait 5: One Nigerian Boy

One Nigerian Boy
www.onenigerianboy.com
Nigeria
Lives in United Kingdom
Launched in 2010
Few words: African, youth, educative, informative, global, pioneering, niche, unique, digital

ONENIGERIANBOY.COM

Name: One Nigerian Boy

URL: www.Onenigerianboy.com

Country of origin: Nigeria

Country of residence: United Kingdom

Launched: 2010

A few words: African. Youth. Educative. Informative. Global. Pioneering. Niche. Unique. Digital.

Portrait 6: Chronique Beauté Noire

Chronique beaute noire
www.chroniquebeautenoire.com
Togo
Lives in France
Launched in 2011
Few words : health, well being, informative, society, diaspora, skin care, beauty, ethnic cosmetics,all public

Name : Chronique Beauté Noire

URL: www.chroniquebeautenoire.com

Country of origin: Togo

Country of residence: France

Launched: 2011

A few words: health, wellbeing, informative, society, diaspora, beauty, ethnic cosmetics, beauty care, for all the public.

Portrait 7: Nana Harmonie

Nana Harmonie s'exprime
www.nanaharmonie.blogspot.com
Congo
Lives in Switzerland
Launched in 2012
Few words: Unique, Harmony, interesting, multicultural, African, Woman, Love , Sparkling,Positive

Name: Nana Harmonie

URL: www.nanaharmonie.blogspot.fr

Country of origin: Congo Brazzaville

Country of residence: Switzerland

Launched: 2012

A few words: unique, harmony, interesting, multicultural, African, women, love, sparkling, positive.

Portrait 8: Cabo Live

Cabo Live
www.cabolive.ch
Cap Verde
Lives in Switzerland
Launched in 2007
Few words: Africa, Cape Verde, Creativity, Marketing, Design, Passion, Beauty, If you know where you are from you know where you are going.

Name: Cabo Live

URL: www.cabo-live.com

Country of origin: Cape Verde

Country of residence: Switzerland

Launched: 2007

A few words: Africa, Cape Verde, Creativity, Marketing, Design, Passion, Beauty, If you know where you are from, you know where you are going.

Portrait 9: Belle Ebène

Belle Ebene
www.bellebene.com
Republic Democratic of Congo and Senegal
Lives in France
Launched in 2008
Few words: tips and sales of cosmetic products for dark and mixed raced skin tones

Name: Belle Ebène

URL: www.belleebene.com

Country of origin: Senegal and RDC

Country of residence: France

Launched: 2008

A few words: tips and sales of cosmetic products for dark and mixed raced skin toned people.

Portrait 10: Black Women in Europe

Black women in Europe
www.blackwomenineurope.com
USA
Lives in England and Sweden
Launched in 2006
Few words:ground-breaking, uplifting, educational,
community-building

Name: Black Women in Europe

URL: www.blackwomenineurope.com

Country of origin: USA

Country of residence: England/Sweden

Launched: 2006

A few words: ground-breaking, uplifting, educational, commu-nity-building

Portrait 11: Made In Africa

MIA Made in Africa
www.mia-culture.com
Democratic Republic of Congo
Lives in Geneva, Switzerland
Launched in 2009
Few words: enthusiastic, convincing, passionate, self-taught, intelligent, cause-related, pioneer, idealistic, strategic

Name: Made in Africa

URL: www.mia-culture.com

Country of origin: DRC

Country of residence: Switzerland

Launched: 2009

A few words: enthusiastic, convincing, passionate, self-made man, intelligent, pioneer, idealist, strategic

Portrait 12: Just Follow Me

Just Follow Me
www.just-followme.com
Democratic Republic of Congo
Liuves in Belgium
Launched in 2011
Few words: Eclectic, Afro-oriented, Contemporary, Culture oriented, Talent search , Passionate, Open-minded, Traveller, Nature

Name: Just Follow me

URL: www.just-followme.com

Country of origin: Democratic Republic of Congo

Country of residence: Belgium

Launched: 2011

A few words: Eclectic, Afro-orientated, Contemporary, Culture orientated, Talent search, Passionate, Open-minded, Traveller, Loves nature.

Portrait 13: Ms Afropolitan

Miss Afropolitan
www.msafropolitan.com
Finland and Nigeria
Lives in United Kingdom
Launched in 2010
Few words: Feminist, pan-African, collaborative, current, thoughtful, empowering, entertaining, healing, probing.

Name: Ms Afropolitan

URL: www.msafropolitan.com

Country of origin: Finland/Nigeria

Country of residence: United Kingdom

Launched: 2010

A few words: Feminist, Pan-African, collaborative, up to date, thoughtful, empowering, entertaining, healing, probing.

Portrait 14: My Afro Week

My AfroWeek
www.myafroweek.com
Togo /Ivory coast and France/Zambia
Lives in France
Launched in May 2011
Few words: agenda, leisure, showcase, afroparisian, lifestyle, information, community,discovery innovative

Name: My Afro Week

URL: www.myafroweek.tumblr.com

Country of origin: France/Zambia and Togo/Ivory Coast

Country of residence: France

Launched: May 2011

About in 9 words: agenda, leisure, showcase, Afro-Parisian, lifestyle, information, community, discovery, innovative.

Portrait 15: Sista Diaspora

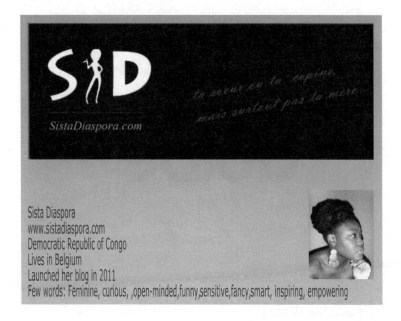

Name: Sista Diaspora

URL: www.sistadiaspora.com

Country of origin: Democratic Republic of Congo

Country of residence: Belgium

Launched: 2011

A few words: feminine, curious, open-minded, funny, sensitive, fancy, smart, inspiring, empowering.

Portrait 16: Africa Fashion Guide

aFrICa//
FaSHION
GUIDE

Africa Fashion Guide
wwwafricafashionguide.com
United Kingdom
Lives in Germany and United Kingdom
Launched in 2011
Few words: -

Name: Africa Fashion Guide
URL: www.africafashionguide.com
Country of origin: United Kingdom
Country of residence: Germany/United Kingdom
Launched: 2011

Portrait 17: Tanya Nefertari

† Φ ▲ **TANYA NEFERTARI** ▲ Φ †

Tanya Nefertari
www.tanyanefertari.com
Zimbabwe
Lives in Manchester (United Kingdom) and Harara (Zimbabwe)
Launched in 2010
Few words:Trendy, Savvy, Africa, Fashion, Design, Afro-Chic, Black Fashion, African Fashion, Exuberant

Name: Tanya Nefertari

URL: www. tanyanefertari.com

Country of origin: Zimbabwe

Country of residence: United Kingdom/ Zimbabwe

Launched: 2010

A few words: Trendy, Savvy, Africa, Fashion Design, Afro-Chic, Black Fashion, African Fashion, Exuberant.

Portrait 18: Louise Sam Photography

Name: Louise Sam Photography

URL: www.louisesamphotography.com

Country of origin: England

Country of residence: England

Launched: 2012

A few words: Explorative, Uplifting, Humorous, Thought-provoking, Inspiring, Awkward, Truthful, Painful, Progressive.

Portrait 19: Invisible cities

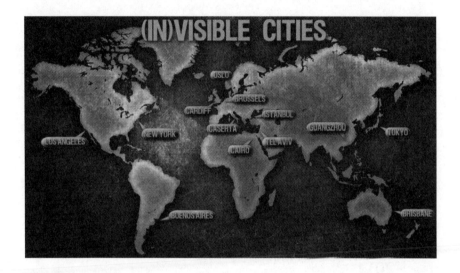

Name: Invisible cities

URL: www.invisiblecities.us

Training: Journalism

Country of origin: Democratic Republic of Congo

Country of residence: Italy

Launched: April 2010

A few words: migration, women, diversity, Black, African, inclusion, journalism, dialogue, collaborative.

Portrait 20: Black Girl in Berlin

Black Girl In Berlin
www.blackgirlinberlin.com
United States
Lives in Berlin
2011
Few words: -

Name: Kimnberlin

URL: www.blackgirlinberlin.com

Country of origin: USA

Country of residence: Germany

Launched: 2011

A few words: personal, honest, revealing, simple

Portrait 21: Go Natural Spain

Go Natural Spain
www.gonaturalspain.com
Dominican Republic
Lives in Madrid
Launched in 2012
Few words: -

Name: Go Natural Spain

URL: www.GoNaturalSpain.com

Country of origin: Dominican Republic

Country of residence: Spain

Launched: 2012

Conclusion

Black beauty, fashion and lifestyle blogging keeps growing up, getting better, earning a stronger presence and gaining greater professionalism. My role as a fashion promoter, a businesswoman and makeup artist has led me to try to see what added value my work may be able to bring to this blogging industry which lacks visibility in the world of mainstream fashion.

Although we have looked at the potential that Black blogging may offer to the most dedicated online platforms, we have also had to consider some of the dangers open to this online world: law enforcement; financial challenges, career development, politics and ethics. We have suggested ways of either to improving the productivity and conversion rate from a blogger to a business owner as well as from a reader to an ethical buyer. A business model freeing bloggers from depending on sponsorships and deals with leading companies is a way of escaping to where most bloggers would like to be. This is, after years of creating a well selected pool of readers, the selling of their online contacts to major beauty and fashion companies. This would be a business model with the potential of educating generations X, Y and Z to behave as conscious consumers, a business model for the 21st century, one that supports trend dissemination, opinion sharing, fashion promotion and the development of beauty icons from an African perspective.

This subjective view on fashion as an industry was motivated by my own professional experience and observations of Black practice of beauty, fashion and lifestyle in London where I live and in Paris where I also follow trends. The core of this book is drawn from my experience of styling and the creative process of reflecting on upcoming trends or the renewal of trends. Understanding why and how Africa has remained outside of the global fashion agenda remained an open question for a while. Trying to answer it has been the most rewarding creative work I have ever undertaken. Thinking about how trends develop and the significance of a location in the context of both migration and the international digital space has led me in several directions. From surveys to interviews, from observation to ethno-photography, each case study and the methods of analyzing it in the context of fashion theory and business' fundamentals underlines the importance of the debate about my ultimate hypothesis: Africa is a credible source of trend creation.

THE END

Glossary

Advertorial: advertisement made through the use of an editorial

Afropean: person of mixed heritage with both European and African origins

Audio-blog: a blog featuring sound

Black European: a black person usually born and raised in Europe

Blogebrity: a person who has become famous for his or her blogging **Blog:** a regularly updated website with information displayed **Blogger:** a writer who specifically use blog posts as medium **Blogging:** updating and writing a blog on a regular basis **Blogosphere:** the blogging world

Blogroll: a side list of other (often related) blogs

CAPICHA: Completely Automated Public Turing test to tell Computers and Humans Apart

Early adopters: people located after a trend has been created and before a trend is widely disseminated

Ecobeauty: ecological beauty

Ecofashion: ecological fashion

Ethical beauty: beauty following ethics including sustainability, fair trading etc

Ethical fashion: fashion following ethics including sustainability, fair trading etc.

Fashion stylist: mood and concept conception and sometimes direction for a photoshoot, fashion show, advertisement or video related to the fashion industry. *See also wardrobe styling.*

Header: a banner placed at the top of a website

HTML: Hyper Text Markup Language, a progam used to format webpages

Keyword: a word or sometimes a sentence likely to be used in search engine

Mblog: a blog updated by mobile phone

Micro-celebrity: online personality often associated with top bloggers

Page views: process of counting how many times a viewer has opened up pages on a blog

Post: a blog entry or update

RSS: Really Simple Syndication, a process often used by bloggers to send updates and new posts to feed-readers

Search engine: a program suggesting a selection of website allocated to certain keywords

SEO: Search Engine Optimisation

Sidebar: a column placed on either side of a blog, permanently visible. The column is often used to place advertising.

Spam: unsolicited comments left on a blog.

Splog: a blog made of spams

Tags: relevant keywords supporting the identification of related posts while aligning them.

Trends: tendency, fashionable habit

Trend circulation: movement followed by the fashionable habit

Trend creation: origin of the fashionable habit

Trend dissemination: tactics and strategies used to enable the circulation of trends

Vlogger: video blogger

Unique visitor count: process of counting how many people visited a blog or a website.

Widget: software which can be installed on a computer to support a blog management

Bibliograpy and sources

Ashton, Sally-Ann (2012), Origin of the Afro comb

African council Switzerland, (2015). Available from: http://www.africancouncil.ch/fr

Archer-Straw, Petrine (2000) Negrophilia: Avant-Garde Paris and Black Culture in the 1920s

Agathine, Sylvain (2014) [Interview by email 27th July 2014] Awondo, Patrick (2014) [Interview by email 7th August 2014]

Awondo, P., Geschiere, P., and Reid, G. (2012) "Homophobic Africa? Toward A More

Nuanced View": Africa Studies Review 55 (3) pp. 145-68

Barger, Jorn (1996). "My Background in AI".

Barthes, Roland, Mythologies (1972) (Hill and Wang, New York)

Barthes, Roland, Elements of Semiology (1968) (Hill and Wang, New York)

Beard, Dafydd (2008), The Branding of Ethical Fashion and the Consumer: A Luxury Niche or

Mass-market Reality?

Bell, David and Kennedy, Barbara (2002), The Cybercultures reader, 2nd edition

Berlin Fashion Week (2015), Available from: http://www.fashion-week-berlin.com/

Berry, Tariq (2007) The Unknown Arabs: Clear, Definitive Proof of the Dark Complexion of the

Original Arabs and the Arab Origin of the so-called African Americans

Bignell, Jonathan (1997). Media semiotics

Birley, Anthony (1972). Septimius Severus: The African Emperor. Garden City: Doubleday

Black History Walks (2014) – talk about the gentrification of Peckham

Bourdieu, Pierre (1979), Distinction

Boateng, Oswald, (2009) Why style matters, BBC4 1st August 2015

Bottomore, T. B. (1964). Elites and society. London, Watts,

Brereton, Bridget (2004) General History of the Caribbean, Volume V: The Caribbean in the

Twentieth Century

Breward, Christopher (2003) Fashion (Oxford History of Art)

Breward, Christopher (1995), The Culture of Fashion: A New History of Fashionable Dress

Breward, Christopher (2006), Fashion's World Cities (Cultures of Consumption Series)

British Museum (2015), West Africa exhibition

British Museum (2015), portraits of Septimius Severus

British Museum (2015), Egypt, Faith after the Pharaohs Exhibition

Brito, Michael. The six Cs. Assessed in 2015. Available from: www.entireweb.com and www.britopian.com

Brooks, David (2001), Bobos in Paradise: The New Upper Class and How They Got There

Brussels city (2015), official website. Available from: www.brussels.be

Buxbau, Greda (1999 & 2005), Icons of fashion, the 20th century

Byron, John (2003), Slavery Metaphors in Early Judaism and Pauline Christianity: A Traditio-Historical and Exegetical Examination

Cavanagh, Allison (2007), Sociology in the age of the Internet

Centre d'information et de promotion d'une nouvelle Afrique (2015). Available from: http://www.cipina.org/preacutesence-africaine-en-suisse.html

Cesaire, Aime (Mai-Juin 1935) numéro 3 de L'Étudiant Noir, Journal Mensuel de l'Association des Étudiants Martiniquais en France

Chalkley, D., Elliott, H. (2014) Return of the Rudeboy exhibition. London, Somerset House

Clarke, Brian (2014) [Interview by Christelle Kedi 22nd July 2014] Clarke, Veronika (2009), Black Nazis

Cohen and Greene (1972), Neither Slave nor free: the Freedom of African descent in the slave societies of the New World, p335-339

Courtin, Philip De Armind (1969), The Atlantic Slave Trade: A Census

Courtin, Philip De Armind (2001), Migration and Mortality in Africa and the Atlantic World,

1700-1900

Courtin, Philip De Armind (1991), The Tropical Atlantic in the Age of the Slave Trade

Cressy, Susan, (2008) Illustrated beauty therapy dictionary

Digital smarts: Protecting your online reputation and safety (2013) Classroom video

Digital smarts: Behaving ethically online (2013) Classroom video

Dalphinis, Morgan (2015), Black Management

Dalphinis, M (1997) New controversial discussions for British Institute of Integrative Psychotherapy Davenport, G. C., and C. B. Davenport. (1909). Heredity of hair color in man. American Naturalist 43: 193-211

Davis, Robert (2004), Christian Slaves, Muslim Masters: White Slavery in the Mediterranean, the Barbary Coast and Italy, 1500-1800

Deumerta, Ana Namibian Kiche Duits: The Making (and Decline) of a Neo-African Language, University of Cape Town. Accessed in 2015. Available from: http://www.mashpedia.com/Namibian_Black_German

Diop, Cheikh Anta (1987), Precolonial Black Africa: a comparative study of the political and social systems of Europe and Black Africa, from antiquity to the formation of modern states.

Diop, Cheikh Anta (1974), The African Origin of Civilization: Myth or Reality

Diop, Cheikh Anta (1978), The Cultural Unity of Black Africa: the domains of patriarchy and of matriarchy in classical antiquity, (Chicago: Third World Press)

Diop, Cheikh Anta (1973) Negro Nations and Culture

Directive commerciale europeenne (mai 2005). **Pratiques commerciales déloyales.** Available from: http://eur-lex.europa.eu/legal-content/FR/TXT/?uri=URISERV%3Al32011

Evening Standard. Deluxe (2014). Assessed on 20th February. "'Pretty girls + nice clothes = big business'"

Exhibition at Maison de l'Afrique (2015) "Pagne de campagne: géopolitique d'un tissu mondial" Paris

Eze, Chielozona (2014) Rethinking African culture and identity: the Afropolitan model (Journal of African Cultural Studies 26 (2), 234-247) Fanon, Frantz (1961), The Wretched of the Earth

Farber, L. (2010). Stepping out in hybrid style: re-negotiating and re-imagining identities in contemporary South African fashion design. Cultural economy in contemporary South Africa: consumption, commodities and media. Guest edited by S Narunsky-Laden. Critical Arts 24(1)

Fashionista.com (2013). Assessed in 2014. Available from: http://www.taymourgrahne.com/artists/hassan-hajjaj

Fausto Boris (1999)A concise history of Brazil, pp. 118-120

Fares, Nabile (1970), Histoire d'une langue. (L'Afrique littéraire et artistique. 17-22)

Fares, Nabile (1972), Littérature orale et anthropologie, these de janvier (Université de Paris X)

Federal Trade Commission (2015). Available from: www.ftc.gov

Food and Drug Administration (2015). Available from: http://www.fda.gov/regulatoryinformation/legislation/federalfooddrugandcosmeticactfdca ct/

Fine, Leah (2007) Colorblind Colonialism? Lusotropicalismo and Portugal's 20th. Century Empire in Africa.

Fogg, Marnie & Steeel Valerie (2013) Fashion: The Whole Story

Freyre, Gilberto (1964), The Masters and the Slaves: A Study in the Development of Brazilian Civilization

Friedmann, John (1986), The world city hypothesis in Development and Change Volume 17, Issue 1, pages 69-83, January 1986

Garance Dore.com (2012). "Career girl Caroline". Available from: http://www.garancedore.fr/en/2012/01/31/career-girl-caroline/ Geoffroy-Schneiter, Berenice (2006), Africa is in Style

Giles, David & Rockwell, Donna, (2009), Being a Celebrity: A Phenomenology of Fame, Journal of Phenomenological Psychology 40 (2):178-210

Godfrey, Brian J., & Zhou, Yu. (1999). Ranking World Cities: Multinational corporations and the global urban hierarchy. Urban Geography, 20(3), 268-281.

Goodwin, Paul (2009), Gentlemen of Bacongo

Greenwood, Norman N.; Earnshaw, Alan (1997). Chemistry of the Elements (2nd ed.) Hackney Museum (2015), African Threads Hackney style exhibition

Hagan, Helen (1993), Tazzla Institute for Cultural Diversity

Hajjaj, Hassan. (2014) [Interview by Christelle Kedi and filmed by Boris Mitkov 14th July 2014] Hall, Stuart (2001), Different.

Hall, Stuart (1993), Cultural identity and Diaspora.

Hall, Stuart (1988), The Windrush Legacy.

Heuman, Gad (2006), The Caribbean (Brief histories)

Hiscock, Jane, Moorman, Nicci and Palmer, Leah. Illustrated Hairdressing Dictionary (2008) Issa, Rose & Hajjaj, Hassan (2014) Photography, Fashion, Film, Design

Jordan, Don & Walsh, Michael A. (2007), The Forgotten History of Britain's White Slaves in America

Karaganis, Joe (2007) Structures of Participation in Digital Cultures

Kanneh, Kandiatu (1998) African Identities: Race, Nation and Culture in Ethnography, Pan-Africanism and Black Literatures

Kaplan, David & Wheeler, James & Holloway, Stephen (2008) Urban Geography

Kaufman, Miranda (2011) PhD thesis "Africans in Britain, 1500-1640

Kedi, Christelle (2013) Beautifying the Body in Ancient Africa and Today (Books of Africa, London)

Kedi, Christelle (2014) interviews with blogger Afroblush

Kedi, Christelle (2015) Femmes, Genres et Corps (Communication pour FIEGED) Kedi, Christelle (November 2013 to February 2014) Focus groups

Kedi, Christelle (March and July 2014) Surveys

Keese, Alexander (2006), Living with Ambiguity, Integrating an African Elite in French and Portuguese Africa, 1930-61,

Kerr, Robert (1844), A general history and collections of travels arranged. (Edinburgh, William Blackwood)

Khumalo NP, Gumedze F (September 2007). "African hair length in a school population: a clue to disease pathogenesis?". Journal of Cosmetic Dermatology 6(3): 144-51.

Kirwan, James (1999), Beauty

Loussouarn, G. (August 2001). "African hair growth parameters". Br. J. Dermatol. 145 (2): 294-7

Maison de l'Afrique (2015), exposition « Pagne de campagne: géopolitique d'un tissu mondial »

McKenna and Pole (2006). Black bloggers and the Blogosphere.

Malaquias, Assis (2000), Ethinicity and conflict in Angola: prospects for reconciliation

Marcniche, Dana R (1991), The African heritage and ethnohistory of the Moors : Background to the emergence of early Berber and Arab peoples, from prehistoryto the Islamic dynasties. in Journal of African Civilizations, Vol II, Fall, pp. 93-150

Marwick, Alice & Boyd, Danah, To See and Be Seen: Celebrity Practice on Twitter (Microsoft Research, USA)

Massaquoi, Hans (1999), Destined to Witness: Growing Up Black in Nazi Germany

Mazon, Patricia (2005). Not So Plain as Black and White: Afro-German Culture and History, 1890-2000. Rochester: University of Rochester Press. pp. 2-3. Merholz, Peter (1999), "Play with your words".

Miano, Leonora (2008), Afropean soul

Mintel (2008) Report on Ethnic Fashion Shopping

Mintel (September 2010), "The Empowered consumer"

Mintel (2008), "Household internet access levels by ethnic group"

Mintel (2012), Social media: Beauty and Personal Care

Mintel (2013), The Ethical Consumer – UK

Morgan, Kenneth (2010), The Oxford History of Britain (revised edition)

Mudimbe, V.Y. (1988), The Invention of Africa. Gnosis, Philosophy, and the. Order of Knowledge (Bloomington, Indiana University Press)

Muller, Florence (2014), « La Parisienne: une figure de mode », Institut Francais de la Mode on 4th September. Available from: http://plus.franceculture.fr/la-parisienne-une-figure-de-mode

Nakamura, Lisa (2006), Cultural difference, theory, and cyberculture studies. (Critical cyber-cultures studies p29-36)

Nielsen report (2011). Available from : www.blog.nielsen.com

Official Tourism office for Portugal (2015). Available from: https://www.visitportugal.com/en/sobre-portugal/biportugal

Organisation Mondiale de la Francophonie (2010) Available from: http://www.francophonie.org/

Oliver, Roland and Atmore Anthony (1967), Africa since 1800

Oliver, Roland and Atmore, Anthony (1981), The African Middle Ages

Pennell, C. R. (2003), Morocco: from Empire to Independence Perier, Gaston-Denys (1930) Les douze travaux du Congophile Perier, Gaston-Denys (1930) Encyclopédie du Congo belge Phit, Miss (2012) Generation Bloggeuses

Plaja, Luisa. The quick expert guide to writing a blog (2012)

Plevin, Julia (2008-08-08). "Who's a Hipster?". Available from: www.huffingtonpost.com

Pole, Antoinette (2005). Blogging the Political: Politics and Participation in a Networked Society

Rashidi, Runoko (1985), The African Presence in Early Asia

Rashidi, Runoko (2012), Black Star: The African Presence in Early Europe (Books of Africa, London)

Reclus, Onesime (1873), Géographie de la France et de ses Colonies Reclus, Onesime (1877), Géographie : La Terre à vol d'oiseau (2 volumes) Reclus, Onesime (1886), France, Algérie et Colonies

Reclus, Onesime (1889), La France et ses Colonies

Respect Mag.com (2012). Available from: http://www.respectmag. com/2012/01/25/afrosomething-lettre-ouverte-au-magazine-elle-5942

Rocamora, Agnès (2009), Fashioning the City: Paris, Fashion and the Media

Rockwell, D. and Giles, D.C. (2009), Being-in-the-world of celebrity: The phenomenology of fame. (Journal of Phenomenological Psychology, 40, 178-210)

Rodriguez, Junius P. (1997), The Historical Encyclopedia of World Slavery, (2 volumes) Sagay, Esi (1984), African Hairstyles: Styles of Yesterday and Today

Schroer, William J. Assessed in (2015), Generations X, Y, Z and the Others. Available from: http://www.socialmarketing.org/newsletter/features/generation3.htm

Scott, D. (2009), The West Indian Front Room: reflections on a Diaspora Phenomenon. (London: Arts Council of Great Britain)

Seed, Patricia (2007), "Navigating the Mid-Atlantic, or What Gil Eanes Achieved", Seeman, Erik R., The Atlantic in Global History, 1500-2000, (Pearson)

Senft, Theresa M. (2008). Camgirls: Celebrity & Community in the Age of Social Networks. (New York: Peter Lang Publishing, Inc).

"Selasi" Tuakli-Wosornu, Taiye (2005). Bye-Bye, Babar (or: What is an Afropolitan?) Slevin, James (2000), The Internet and Society

Shillington, K. (2004) Encyclopedia of African History 3-Volume Set

Silver, David and Massanari, Adrienne (2006), Critical Cyber Culture Studies

Soboye, Samson (2014) [Interview by Christelle Kedi March 2014] Soboye boutique (2015). Available from : http://soboye.tictail. com/

Soral, Alain, Camus, Renaud, Dustan, Guillaume and Sevran, Pascal (2002), Débat sur le communautarisme gay (LCI)

Strauss, William & Howe, Neil (2000). Millennials Rising: The Next Great Generation

Taymour Grahne gallery (2015). "Hassan Hajjaj". Available from: http://www.taymourgrahne.com/artists/hassan-hajjaj

Tecnorati.com (2015). Available from: www.technorati.com

The Guardian on 12th September 2011. Available from: http://www. theguardian.com/commentisfree/2011/sep/12/portugal-race

The Guardian on 11th December 2014. Available from: http://www. theguardian.com/books/2014/dec/11/zoella-ghostwriter-sioban-curham-controversy-childrens-author

The Telegraph on 26th November 2014. Available from: http:// www.telegraph.co.uk/news/uknews/law-and-order/11255077/ Hidden-advertising-by-vloggers-under-the-spotlight.html

Thompson, John B. (1995), The Media and Modernity: A Social Theory of the Media. (Stanford: Stanford University Press)

Tulloch, Carol (2004), Black British Style Exhibition tour

Van Wyk, C. (2006) Gay subculture – a study of consumer behaviour and its implications for marketing communications

Verger, Pierre (1951) Congo-Belge (DRC), photographies

Walker, Robin (2006) When we ruled

WGSN.com (2015). Available from: www.wgsn.com

Web designer wall (2015). 7 web design trends to watch. Available from; http://webdesignerwall.com/trends/7-web-design-trends-to-watch-for-in-2015

Whitaker Report, United Nations (1985)

Wolfenden Report, Departmental Committee on Homosexual Offences. (1957)